Seems Like Old Times

D1375538

Seems Like Old Times

A Year in the Life of

Alan Coren

 Robson Books

First published in Great Britain in 1989 by Robson Books Ltd,
Bolsover House, 5-6 Clipstone Street, London W1P 7EB
This Robson paperback edition first published 1991

British Library Cataloguing in Publication Data
Coren, Alan, 1938-
    Seems like old times: a year in the life of Alan Coren.
    I. Title
    828'.91408

ISBN 0-86051-599-0 (cased)
ISBN 0-86051-736-5 (pbk)

Printed in Hungary

A SANDAL IN BOHEMIA

About a year ago, I gave up executive life, threw a toothbrush, a word processor and a case of Glenlivet into a red-spotted bandanna, and struck out for Bohemia.

I did not need the toothbrush. Bohemia turned out to lie just beyond the front gate. You could wander that chartless wonderland at will, fetch up against the most bizarre of its inhabitants, poke about in its most peculiar crannies, embroil yourself in the most marginal of its cultural quirks, find yourself experiencing its dottiest events and conversations, and still get back to Cricklewood in time for *Neighbours*.

What follows is a spatchcock journal of that insouciant meander. Originally sent back to *The Times* as weekly despatches from the shifting front, it has undergone a little hindsighted tinkering, an afterthought there, a link here, but nothing has been done, I think, to diminish its consistent inconsistency, because that is what life is like.

At least, one year's worth of it unquestionably was.

AC

JUNE

Middle is a dispiritingly practical age. There is a tendency to sift through unfulfilled dreams and begin chucking out the wilder ones, because they are never going to be any use to you, and to be sensible about making room in the dwindling attic of possibility for just a few of the tamer numbers. I no longer, for example, expect to be asked to make up a four for the North face of the Eiger, or to have the dividing door of my Inverness sleeper burst open, precipitating a sloe-eyed heiress into my bunk.

I have become a little too overweight for the Aintree course, and a little too myopic for Malcolm Marshall's short-pitched stuff; and, since this is the best prose-style I can muster, I recently put a bracket-clock in that space on the mantelpiece hitherto reserved for the Nobel Prize.

At about the same time, I also jettisoned the oldest dream I owned. I had had it for over forty years, and there was clearly no point in hanging on to it when I needed the space for a more sensible item—in this instance, a fantasy in which I find a shower that keeps the same temperature throughout—so I junked it. And, wouldn't you know, no sooner had I done so than I suddenly needed to lay my hands on it.

In the spring of 1944 I was sitting on Blackpool beach and wondering whether there was anything worse to be than a five-year-old evacuee when so major a shadow passed over me that for a moment I thought that God had finally done as nightly requested and arrived to take me back to London.

I looked up, and was not immediately disabused: while the shadow wasn't God—because even at five I knew that God didn't have twin engines—that wasn't to say that the plane it belonged to mightn't have had God at the controls. Not only was it the most beautiful plane I had ever seen, it could perform miracles. Ten seconds later, it landed in the sea. It didn't sink. It walked on water.

It was a Catalina. It looked like a steel gull. It had a 100ft wingspan and the body of a racing launch. I learned a lot about it in the next few days, because I had never wanted to know as much about anything before. Not only could it fly 4,000 miles without refuelling and land on water, it could also land on land, because it was amphibian.

It was the best vehicle there had ever been. If you had a Catalina, everything was possible. There was nowhere you couldn't go, and nothing you couldn't do when you got there. Getting into a Catalina was equivalent to Clark Kent's walking into a phone booth. Until puberty came along to interfere, the Catalina was the only thing worth dreaming about.

I never saw one again. Grown, but still preoccupied with the idea of flying one, I would make inquiries and be told they had all been scrapped. There would be occasional rumours, Yeti-like, to the effect that one had been sighted carrying mail in the Solomons, another was joyriding around the Canadian lakes, and so on, but they never came to anything. So, eventually, I yielded the dream to the bin.

It is no coincidence that *Some Enchanted Evening* was written for a middle-aged glottis. On February 24, 1988, I saw a stranger across a crowded room, and somehow I knew. In that peristaltic shuffling common to all cocktail parties, I eventually fetched up against him, and he introduced himself as Dr Alan Borg, Curator of the Imperial War Museum. We talked of this and that, and inevitably at last, of the other.

He smiled. He had every right to. He knew where to find a Catalina.

10

Last Sunday was an extraordinary day. Last Sunday knew I was coming. Stir pathetic fallacy into nostalgia and you have as intoxicating a brew as you can shake a joystick at. Not only does Duxford Aerodrome, active wing of the Imperial War Museum, lie in flattest Cambridgeshire, where the landscape is 10 per cent earth and 90 per cent sky, so that nature seems to have established the apt priorities, but the weather itself appeared to have been restored, like Duxford's veteran aircraft, to mint 1940 condition.

Last Sunday, you could lie on the warm grass airstrip from which Bader once took off and look past the propeller of a Spitfire hub-deep in daisies and see vapour trails diffusing themselves into the blue. You could smell Lancaster on the breeze, and feel your fillings resonate to piston-engined harmonics, a dental treat I had not savoured in decades. Jets don't do it.

The Catalina stood on the apron, four-dimensional: if I narrowed my eyes, I could see Blackpool Pier behind it. Braced for the disappointment of finding it less than I had either remembered or imagined, I had never guessed that finding it so much more would leave me flummoxed: the machine had the kind of beauty which transcended sentimentality.

You could look at it objectively and reflect that it was only technology which had made it obsolete; had it been a question solely of aesthetics, aeronautical design could have stopped right there. This was as beautiful as a plane was ever going to be.

So we took it up, and it flew like a tractor, but it didn't matter a damn.

If you have change, prepare to lose it now. There are three days of the Grosvenor House Antiques Fair left to go, and—contrary to the glum maunderings of nostalgics who bang on about the good old days when it was possible to nip down to Park Lane, have a slap-up fish tea, buy a little table and a rug to put under it and a carriage clock to stand on it and a mirror to hang behind it and still have change out of a million pounds—bargains abound. Now is a good time to buy. Dealers who have flocked thither from all over the queendom are loath to wrap everything up again and bung it back on the handcart, and will, as rickety spinets prepare to take a terminal crack at *Auld Lang Syne*, haggle.

Yesterday, for example, I could have snapped up a nice little Boudin, at least 9 inches by 16 and never had a spanner on it. for £275,000. Better yet, there was 10 per cent off a very appealing T'ang horse which would have looked a treat standing on a similarly discounted English two-drawer commode, and you could have taken the pair away for a quarter of a million.

The Grosvenor House experience is quite peculiar. It is not really a fair at all, in the strictest sense—by which I do not mean that it is short of coconuts and dying goldfish, rather that it does not fulfil the primary function of a fair to be a convocation of dealers buying and selling to one another. That has already been done at all the other fairs of which Grosvenor is the distillation and apogee: the Delft posset pot or Sheraton carver which started the year at some country house sale for ten grand and, by acquiring the rich patina which comes from being passed from sweaty hand to sweaty hand, arrives at Grosvenor House six months later at double the price, has come to the end of its professional career. It is now ripe for sale to a civilian punter.

True, a little last-ditch interactive trading still goes on by dealers not entirely exhausted by adding noughts to labels, to whom it suddenly occurs that the bloke on the neighbour stall has not quite squeezed the ultimate drop out of an item's market potential, and who sprint round with it covertly scribbling on the price tag as they run, but this is rare. Grosvenor House is the opportunity for people like you and me, and anyone else with a Lear jet for commuting between yachts, to furnish our niches.

How bizarre it is to see a sales ticket with five zeros on it! How fraught with delightful ironies to overhear a dealer explain that a Georgian break-front bookcase was £10,000 more than it might otherwise have been expected to fetch because it came with its original workshop bill for seven guineas! How pleasantly voyeuristic to watch that same customer unsheath his cheque book without another gasp and nonchalantly jot a sum upon which most of us would happily retire, content to shelve our books on something solid from John Lewis. Grosvenor House is a testing spot to loiter. You may, for example, test your soul for envy. The likelihood, gratifyingly, is that you will find yourself not to be experiencing it. The rarity of the goods and the comic magnitude of the prices—you really do turn the labels over and feel the mouth begin to curve, willy-nilly, upwards—combine to distance them from any possibility which might excite jealousy. The fantasy which might encourage you to covet that Breughel falls apart when invited to suggest a place to hang it. You could easily grow to dislike an old Chinese jug which was worth more than your house. You could well find yourself shouting at it when the time came to retile the roof and you didn't have the cash.

More usefully, and far more unsettlingly, you may test your taste. If you have reached your middle years and reckon yourself a citizen with a good eye, Grosvenor House can play strange tricks on your aesthetic smugness. A primitive painting of a bloated pig with funny little legs, an inlaid ebony writing-box which even my untrained eye could spot was already growing disturbingly outlaid, a wonky fireside chair so constructed as to keep an osteopath in regular employment, an asexual porcelain midget with a absent foot, a Venetian mirror boasting glass so original that long minutes might be spent attempting to decipher your own nose in the khaki gloom—that these may add up to £96,000 is a severe test of one's connoisseurship.

Nor is the fair to be ignored as a useful place for examining one's understanding of one's fellow man. Not, mind, to increase it. I saw a Japanese gentleman—dressed in the shiny demob suit of a far taller bloke—cough up £60,000 for a tiny translucent bowl, and, while the dealer wrapped it, take from his pocket a creased cigarette stub, and relight it. On the stand of Alistair Sampson Antiques, I observed an elderly English lady measure herself against the carved wooden figure of an 18th-century buck, some four feet and £17,000 high, and mystifyingly murmur to her husband that it was too tall for the dog. At the jewellery display of Harvey & Gore, an American matron, much taken with a turquoise suite but bemoaning the fact that it would not be best suited to brown eyes, pondered aloud, and seriously, whether

13

contact lenses were obtainable in turquoise.

Never miss the Grosvenor House Antiques Fair, even if all you collect is people.

It is not, of course, the All England Tennis Championships at all. It is the All England Vicarage Tea Party. It is the Platonic vicarage tea party of which all others are derivatives, and that is what makes it All English in the first place; for the vicarage tea party is a cultural benchmark. It is one of the few pinpointable essences of England. It is what English soldiers and policemen and politicians and journalists compare things to when they wish succinctly to stress what they are not.

On Tuesday, conditions were exemplary. The sun was beige, the air liquescent, beyond the spire on the hill far thunder mumbled, and, as I stood on the Wimbledon greensward examining a limp cucumber triangle for midges while floral frocks and creased linen jackets milled about me, one of the former murmured to one of the latter: 'Didn't I tell you we should have brought the chairs in?' Rattigan would have hung three acts under that.

Because it is the All English Vicarage Tea Party, it matters not a jot that our boys and girls lose. On the contrary, good manners require them to. Having invited all those nice foreign children over to play, not to mention our own far-flung colonials, it would be awfully bad form to beat them. Jeremy, go and put your shorts on and give that gloomy Czech boy a game, he isn't talking to anybody and he hasn't touched his jelly, no I can't remember his name, it has a lot of -ovs or -vitches in it, but he'll know what you mean if you sort of point to him and wave your bat about a bit.

Strolling the walkways between the outside courts, one is struck by the physical differentials between ours and theirs. Where the domestic young are tripe-white, the foreign young are honey-hued; where ours are soft, theirs are sinewy; where ours smile, theirs snarl; where ours are coltish, theirs are tigerish. Teenage Americans, as they wait, totally tensed, to receive service, look like pop-up plates from some anatomy textbook:

14

their very elbows are muscled; their earlobes flex. The young Slavs have obviously been put together on assembly lines in Brno and Sofia, so clearly defined are the taut components which have been strung and bolted by state ergonometrists grafting late into the night, while Igor prowls the trembling villages in search of yet more serviceable bits.

Ours are players, theirs are athletes, some would say. Others, perhaps, that ours are human beings, theirs machines. When shall we get a hero, then? Not a valiant struggler, fortuitously upsetting the odds on Court 136 when his opponent, just released from traction, serves enough double faults to allow the Englishman to muddle through into the second round on a wave of embarrassed patriotic clapping, but someone who, on a mere rumour of his imminence, can magnetize the entire vicarage garden, empty its furthest sponsored marquee, scatter a strawberry queue that has patiently been shuffling forwards for hours, persuade each and every debentured drunk to drop his goblet and stagger towards the sound of the guns?

On Tuesday afternoon, as I was slowly wheezing up the staircase towards the Centre Court for the Wilander-Masso match, I was suddenly aware of a hysterical army bounding at my heels; who, having caught up with me, bore me along in shrieking urgency. I had to go where they went. My feet were off the concrete. Patently, Wilander, Number 2 seed and Grand Slam candidate, was more charismatic than reputation had hitherto allowed; nice ticket to have, I thought, when until then I hadn't thought anything of the sort, and gripped it the more tightly against ambush.

I need not have worried. Instead of turning, at the top of the steps, right towards the Centre Court, my roaring caravan swung left towards Court Number One. It was packed to the gunwales, and my mob being thus unable to get in, could only fight, literally, to get close, pressing into the mob already jammed against the corridor windows, cheeks flattened to the hot glass, limbs pinioned, and the packed hearts beating so near and so hard that the communal tachycardia made your fillings rattle.

He did not appear for ten more minutes, while the crescent buzz spiralled the pigeons and flaked the rust off the corrugated roof. Then the tuckets, then the trumpets, then the cannon, and he comes!

It might have been Lenin riding back on the cowcatcher of the 8.14 or Douglas MacArthur wading ashore on New Guinea to fulfil his pledge, but it was more than either of these. It was J.P. McEnroe, back to claim his birthright; and 40,000 people would have followed him anywhere. Indeed . . . glimpsing from beneath an alien armpit his anabasis . . . when I saw him neither smile nor nod nor speak but merely raise one forearm in Roman salute, I could not help thinking it a bit of a waste of good honest idolatry to squander it on a mere first-round tennis match. All things considered, it seemed rather a pity that the Sudetenland wasn't still up for grabs.

Personally, mind, I felt it was all a trifle over the top. If this sort of thing isn't curbed, and jolly quickly too, I may well send a stiff note to the vicar.

Beware pathetic fallacy. Man's confident assumption that his environment is so sympathetic to his moods as to kick in with complementary props when he requires them bespeaks the kind of arrogance that invites come-uppance. Indeed, language having deteriorated somewhat since Ruskin's smug nib jotted the sneer, it has taken on even more satisfyingly sarcastic resonances. 'What did you think of that fallacy, Brian?' 'Pathetic, Harry!'

Let us take, then, the night when there were six Aston Martins in serried rank beneath the pine trees at La Baule. No ordinary night, either, last Monday, but the very eve of my 50th birthday, cusp and watershed both, with much to occupy the few remaining brain cells still ticking beneath the vanished thatch.

We had chosen La Baule with great care: it is an excellent refuge when one is fleeing 1988, a spot virtually unchanged from its Thirties heyday when the Hispano-Suizas and Isotta-Fraschinis beetled down to South Brittany with, if not the crowned, at least the coroneted nobs of Europe lolling on the rear banquettes and pawing something fetching in a cloche hat as prelude to the weekend's consummations. While, from the north, the Aston Martins, taking a break from the punishing routines of Cliveden and Fort Belvedere, descended to park beside them on the forecourt of the Hotel Hermitage, for baccarat and dalliance and fresh foie gras.

So we put up, when I was 49, at l'Hermitage, and we took a balconied room that faced the sunset and there was nothing about this elegant Edwardian pile to suggest that 1938 was not still with us. We booked for dinner at Le Castel Marie-Louise, which not only serves the finest tucker in all Brittany but serves it in an ambience that invites one to crane discreetly for a glimpse of Wallis Simpson poking about in a lobster. It is a restaurant where the only frozen stuff is time; a very good place to be 49.99 years of age. And it was here that, as we strolled through its gate, we saw the Astons drawn up on the lawn beneath the pines. Not any old Astons, either, but the best Astons of all, the 1.5-litre Le Mans tourers, 1930s legends of style, engineering and performance so ineffably English that those of us who fancy cars instinctively know, though Wodehouse didn't specify, that when Bertie asked Jeeves to bring the two-seater round to the front, there was no question of what Jeeves would come round to the front in.

I may have gasped. Certainly, something disturbed the susurrus rhythm in the trees, but it could have been the ghost of some old sportsman, haunting the places where his honour died.

The cars were all in pristine scarlet, spotless, shimmering; setting sunbeams winked off the burnished chromium. Since all had British number-plates, and since a knot of drinkers stood a few yards off among the marigolds, loosing arcane jargon into the evening air, it wasn't difficult to put six and six together. We walked across. How could we not? Fate had brought them here to trill the grace notes on my nostalgia, and though the risk was there that they would turn out to be merely ostentatious fanciers of statusful ironmongery or shrewd investors in the vintage market or, yet worse, dodgy dealers conspiring to separate from their francs those well-heeled Frenchmen eager for *quelque chose de grand snob*, it was a risk that had to be run.

I need not have worried. They were romantics all. Specialist romantics, indeed; not merely, as one might loosely have assumed, The Aston Martin Club, but The One-And-A-Half-Litre Le Mans Aston Martin Club, the happy few, and they had chosen La Baule for their rendezvous, because, well, what more reverberant backdrop could there be than this spot only a hundred miles from Le Mans itself, essentially unchanged from the days when the original drivers of cars like these had repaired thither to recuperate from 24 hours of aching forearms and oily eyes and desiccated lips?

And yet, and yet. Fate has two hands. She is not all give. Even as the cheery buffs and I strolled back towards their cars, to enable them to point out this structural nuance and that, my pitiable glee at the remarkable tonal consistency of it all was running out of time. I asked the wrong question.

'Sad, isn't it,' I said, 'that old cars aren't like other antiques?'

They looked at me.

'Old furniture,' I said, 'pictures, porcelain, silver, old books, coins, all that – given reasonable care, they'll last more or less forever. Whereas old cars . . .'

'Will do exactly the same,' said a buff, firmly. The other buffs nodded.

'There is nothing,' said the first buff, 'to prevent these from being preserved infinitely.'

'Oh good,' I said.

I did my best, of course, to look pleased. Just as if the curator, say, of the V & A were to point out to me that the figures on the Grecian urn we happened to be passing would remain forever panting and forever young. There was no earthly reason why anyone else should have concerned himself that I should be 50 in three hours, and that the odds of being preserved infinitely suddenly seemed somewhat long.

18

JULY

The pillar box on the corner has been closed, and thereby hangs a puzzle. Not as to why it has been closed; that is clear from the printed label gummed askew beneath the ex-slot. Due to industrial action, it says, this box is closed. Fine. I accept that. The puzzle of the postal strike itself is not the one I wish to address, since it is bound to be an imponderably complex little number, fraught with the minutiae of haggle and nuance; you can tell that from the way it has been simmering for years, suddenly flaring up and just as suddenly flaring down again.

It is not unlike acne, except that it always seems to start in Harrow-on-the-Hill. Don't ask me why; it could be a singularly offensive sort of junk mail they have there; a particularly malevolent breed of local dog, perhaps. It could be cackling Harrovians dropping bags of flour on postmen from their privileged crenellations. I do not know why Harrow breeds postal militancy, but that's where it always seems to start, and next day NW1 has gone down with it, and the day after that you wake up in Cricklewood with all your slots bolted.

It is the slot-bolting which is the puzzle. It represents an unfathomable admixture of skill and ineptitude; at once professional and amateur, considered and impromptu, official and anarchic. It could well be a metaphor of some kind – you can feel its cryptic message even while you recognise that it will ever elude you.

21

The pillar-box slot is curved and lipped. A great deal of thought has gone into its design; you can tell that ergonomists and aesthetes and meteorologists and accountants have sat down and collaborated long and hard to arrive at the ideal slot, and that is what we now have. I speak as one who has committed letters to most of the world's postal systems, usually gingerly, and I have to tell you that there is nothing that offers a more agreeable receptacle than the British pillar-box, largely because of its slot. Just something about it.

No such creative deliberation, however, has gone into the thing which, in time of industrial dispute, is bolted over the slot. Not only is it not bevelled for maximum snugness, it is not even curved. It is a crude iron oblong. It is wonky. It does not fit the slot.

All right, you counter, why should it? It does its job. It stops letters getting poked in. It is not a designer-obstacle, but an improvised afterthought, a rough but honest barrier expressing solidarity with the downtrodden masses, doubtless beaten from a simple iron ingot by the horny but untrained hands of postmen hammering in their own time, while their plucky women sat by a single candle invisibly mending their man's fanged trousers, or sponging flour from their hats.

Wrong. If you care to examine the obstacle, you will see that it has a bolt through it; no ordinary bolt, either. By wiggling the ill-fitting obstacle aside, not enough to shove a letter through, of course, but enough to take an informative squint, you will see that this bolt goes right across the diameter of the pillar-box, and fits snugly into a machined seating on the far side. Furthermore, the bolt is furnished at its external end not by one of those mundane little channels susceptible to the common screwdriver but by two peculiar little conical indentations which unquestionably require a Special Tool with which to tighten the bolt.

It is, patently (probably in every sense), a calculatedly designed and expertly engineered bolt. It has been thought out. More significantly, there is every indication that it was part of the integral design of the box itself – which, I note from the façade, was commissioned for the corner of my street by the extremely late King George.

In short, when they built the box all those years ago, the Post Office obviously anticipated the contingencies of industrial strife. They knew that talks entered into in a frank and free spirit seeking genuine compromise would irremediably break down due to, there is no other word for it, one side's intransigence. They knew that the offer on the table would be deemed derisory. They knew that the democratic right to deploy the only weapon in the embittered employees' arsenal would be, albeit regretfully, exercised. And they themselves provided the means for bunging up the slot. That strikes me as exceedingly odd.

Unless, of course, the Post Office was in fact playing a remarkably cunning game. Might the clue to it lie in the very crudity of the obstructing device when compared with the sophistication not only of the box itself but also of the means of securing the blockage? Did, that is, the Founding Fathers of the Post Office calculate, in their infinite deviousness, that nothing more infuriates a customer than running down to catch the last delivery and finding a chunk of iron wedged, ostensibly amateurishly but undeniably effectively, between him and his addressee, with a gummed note to the effect that the union is up to its old tricks again?

In an otherwise pretty comprehensive roster of fringe crackpottery mustered for today's Kensington by-election, the absence of an Anti-Carriage-Drive Tendency candidate strikes me as, quite frankly, astonishing. Is there no one in that hitherto maniacally conservationist constituency prepared to cough up £500 for the opportunity of banging on publicly about the grisly despoliation of our heritage by loose chipping and reproduction urn?

Once, the plump bourgeois villas of Kensington and other pleasant inner suburbs were aproned by green lawns girt with privet and punctuated by hydrangea bush and hybrid tea. But over the past few years these have been systematically replaced by oxblood-coloured tarmac forecourts horribly planted with polystyrene tubs and BMWs. What makes this ruin especially irritating is that most of these large houses have garages so it is clearly not a question of necessary off-street parking. The question it is clearly of is display. The carriage-drive is not for carriage-driving on, it is for carriage-parking on. It is for sticking the 450SEL in, behind the Audi Estate, with the 944 Turbo bringing up the rear. This says more about you than geraniums ever can.

I have nothing against German ironmongery, but it is not, God wot, a lovesome thing, and I am deeply disappointed that the caring folk of Kensington, who once campaigned so successfully against the bin-liner mountain, have not found a champion for this yet worthier cause.

S till, the well-heeled do have their own special crosses to bear. More and more these days, I find myself having to disengage from fascinating conversations about the difficulty of finding decent plumbers in Antibes, or the gratifying boom in post-Impressionist prices, and stroll outside for a breath of fresh air. So, puzzled by what I observe to be an unhappily increasing social hazard, I telephoned my dentist to inquire why it was that the rich appeared to be developing bad breath.

'Jacket crowns,' he said instantly.

'Aha,' I said, as if I understood.

'Yes,' he said, as if he guessed I didn't. 'Twenty years ago, there was, among those who could afford it, a vogue for full mouth reconstruction. They paid £5,000, and we rebuilt their heads. We filed their existing teeth to pegs, and we fitted impeccable surrogates in their place.'

'Hardly impeccable,' I countered, 'if the net effect was halitosis capable of de-scaling a kettle at fifty paces.'

'Not our fault,' he snapped. 'Patients were warned that unless they were assiduous in cleaning their prostheses where they joined the gum, the long-term prognosis indicated periodontal decay. That, I am afraid, is what is now happening. It must be very worrying for them.'

'Uneasy lies the head that wears a crown,' I murmured.

'I don't find that even mildly amusing,' he said.

Like many people who did not, at a critical stage in their lives, seize the opportunity to toss a few essentials into a carpet-bag, ship aboard a rusting scow, and head for a satisfying career combing the beaches of Tahiti, I find myself, today, attending lots of business meetings.

Since it would obviously be ungraciousness itself to make this plea specifically and face-to-face, may I suggest generally, and in the public interest, that a current buzz-phrase be dropped from the executive lexicon before someone sitting opposite me gets felled with a Perrier bottle?

The phrase is, 'I hear what you say.'

Its sub-text (hidden agenda?) is, of course, anything from 'but it is a load of codswallop' to 'and I intend doing sod-all about it'. I should normally have let it die a natural death, as such bits of tacky gobbledegook are prone to do, had I not been at a media-folk meeting last week when one man said, 'I hear what you say' to the man next to him, and the man next to him thought for a bit, and replied 'I hear what you say' back. It was then that I decided something had to be done.

Lumbering athletically about the tennis court on Monday, I noticed that my backhand had suddenly become even more unpredictable, in that whenever I played the shot I shrieked in agony and dropped my racquet. However, since the membership of my club is of a vintage which spends most of its sporting life in traction, names of reliable physiotherapists were being shouted across the greensward even as I crumpled. I hobbled home, changed, selected the nearest address – which just happened to be in Wigmore Street – and hailed a cab.

He pulled up outside an Edwardian mansion block. 'Would you mind waiting?' I said. 'I shan't be long.'

He looked at me. I pressed the brass bell push, and an unnecessarily stunning girl in a white frock opened the door. After about 20 minutes of pummelling and ultrasound, she let me out again.

'Anyone famous in today?' said the cabdriver.

'What?'

'Polo players, Frank Bough, royalty, catch my drift?'
'I've hurt my arm,' I said, coldly.
'Doesn't surprise me,' he said, and let in the clutch.

When Noël Coward encouraged Elyot Chase to cry 'Strange, how potent cheap music is!' he did not mean the words to be taken literally. Had he so intended, then *Private Lives* would have been set on a balcony in Cricklewood, and Elyot's observation would have invited the imperishable riposte, 'Very flat, Wembley'.

Suburban topologists and acousticians will already be ahead of me, but the rest of you will need to be teleported back to last Saturday and set down beside a darkling pond in NW2. A man is shining a flashlight into it because he thinks a world record is about to be broken, but it is a world record which comes out only at night. It is while he is so engaged that he becomes aware of a series of low rhythmic concussions, distant whumps and crumps that are not so much heard as felt. And do you know what this fool – just for a long preposterous moment – thinks?

As his gooseflesh rises, he registers (partly because he has been reading about it earlier in the day) that this is the 72nd anniversary of the Battle of the Somme. And recalls that, in July 1916, gentlemen in England then abed caught on the wind the terrible sound of the barrage opening up 200 miles away in Flanders. Is this, then, some spectral commemoration, far ghosts tugging on their lanyards, lest we forget?

No. The next moment is soberer. The man's son ambles into the garden in search of folding money (for it is Saturday night) and, asked if he can hear anything, reveals – with the sarcastic tut of youth – that the source is Michael Jackson's Wembley concert, six miles away as the decibel flies.

Which, in the third moment, prompts a thought almost as fanciful as the first. If it is flat between me and Wembley, it is even less interrupted for sound going straight up. Will, a million sound-years hence, things on Pluto cock whatever passes for their ears and wonder what these curious signals mean?

The world record? Oldest Tadpole. Four months ago I brought a bucket of frog spawn back from a Cockfosters safari. The tadpoles hatched a fortnight later. By now, according to every known amphibian authority, they should not only be hopping about on the little islands I have so thoughtfully provided, but having a go at croaking.

Mine do not even have legs. They are the size of thumbs, but they are still tadpoles. They have eaten all the weed, and driven off the goldfish, which they go for in packs, like piranha. They are clearly violent antisocial adolescent delinquents with no intention of maturing into adult responsibility. They are Hell's Tadpoles. By day, they hang around in the murk at the bottom of the pond, and at night they swagger out in search of bother. The Saturday cannot be too far off when they come and ask me for folding money.

Will I have the bottle to refuse?

Refusing television offers is even harder. (*That, by the way, was what we broadcasting megastars call a link, and as these things go, consider yourselves to have got off lightly. I might well, given the concluding word of the preceding gobbet, have gone on to discuss garbage disposal*).

I do very little television, and most of it is quite awful. It is probably because it is quite awful, of course, that I am invited to do very little of it, but when the optimistic folk who peddle our fireside opium do ring up, it is very difficult to turn them down, because (a) their voices – in Fitzgerald's imperishable phrase – are full of money, and (b) one forgets – in another of his corkers – their capacity for the casual destruction of ordinary people, in this case oneself. Furthermore (like Gatsby, indeed) one continues to pursue the green light: tomorrow we will run faster, stretch out our arms further . . .

Which is why, on Tuesday evening in Birmingham, I found myself smirking my way through fake French windows onto the cardboard set of yet another new chat show, to be greeted by the eponymous host Jimmy Greaves, and his other guests Britt Ekland, Kim Wilde and Stan Boardman. It was not unlike a play by Wedekind or Sartre. Had it been on stage instead of on

27

television, the audience might quickly have found itself up to his knees in desperate interpretations as to why an ex-footballer, a mature starlet, a stand-up comic, a millionaire pop-singer and a literary hack should have been imprisoned in a fake kitchen, doomed to laugh and natter meaninglessly until someone came and put the lights out. Why did the footballer walk through an artificial front door in one shirt and appear on the other side in a different one? Why was there a picture of Sir Winston Churchill on the wall and a cryptically incomplete set of Arthur Mee's *Children's Encyclopaedia* in the bookcase? Why did the five prisoners suddenly disappear, to be replaced by four young men rising from dry-ice to fill this bizarre kitchen with mimed music?

What did it all mean?

On one level, of course, it meant four hundred quid. But beyond that it remains, even to me, something of a mystery.

Hurtling between ironmongers last Saturday, calling for a clock key – for which there was, of course, no call – it was suddenly borne in upon me that a major source of energy had disappeared from our lives. Clockwork has gone.

Time was, time was clockwork, and so was so much else. Not only was the queendom full of men with ladders and brass cranks pedalling about to ensure the town halls, churches, schools and railway stations kept reasonable pace with Greenwich and did not startle us with errant bongs, but umpteen domestic appliances and toys took their cheery energy from the uncoiling spring, and could generally be relied upon to do so, albeit somewhat briefly. They did not go flat. There were no monitory labels advising us that clockwork was not included. We were not required to dig constantly for the imperial equivalent of £3.99 to feed the insatiable habits of our mechanical helpmeets. And when the clockwork items conked out, men in brown coats mended them. If you take today's batteried equivalent to a man in a brown coat, he throws it in a bin and sells you another one.

But beyond mere convenience, clockwork imposed a discipline all its own. It was a moral force. It demanded reciprocal regularity. There were times of day when you wound things, and special ways of winding them, and slackness or ineptitude invited disorder that spread far beyond the device itself. Tristram Shandy's father, you may recall, was reminded of his nocturnal duty towards Mrs Shandy only by the act of winding the hall clock.

The culture is the poorer – and the more vulnerable – for its passing.

I am being pursued by M Daniel Besseiche of Honfleur, who has a picture in his possession. A copy of it arrived in Monday morning's post, but he has the original, and he is after a considerable amount of folding money.

Let me quickly say that the picture was not snapped through an unnoticed jalousie on some wayward afternoon when calvados eroded inhibition. It is not of me. The picture is a gouache of a Norman boulangerie, plus tree out back and evocative sky, hauntingly painted, and not unreasonably priced at 10,000 francs, all major credit cards accepted. As I discovered when I uncircumspectly wandered into M Besseiche's appealing gallery a month ago, and made the mistake of looking at it.

M Besseiche was on me like a ferret. Within seconds I had been persuaded to admit that it was not only the finest picture I had ever seen but also the biggest bargain. It would, I cried, be the work of a scant minute to sprint to my hotel and prise my traveller's cheques from beneath the floorboards.

Naturally enough, I kept going. Nevertheless, somehow the assiduous M Besseiche has sniffed out my domestic whereabouts – I have always known it to be a mistake to fill in those *fiches d'arrivée*, especially in small towns – and has written to suggest that when he next comes to Britain, he will not turn up empty-handed.

Tuesday's post was much less dispiriting. My dreams of a major musical career are about to be fulfilled. I have been invited to play in a 'personality concert' in aid of cancer research, to the astute organisers of which has clearly come wind, as it were, of my musical polymathy. Flatteringly confident of a universally

29

competent lip, they have despatched a generous letter offering me as wide a choice of instrument as ever came the way of Roland Kirk.

They are not wrong. With a talent like mine, selection will not be difficult. Given the proffered options of blowing down a scaffold tube, watering can, curtain rod, hollow bamboo stalk, car exhaust, toilet roll or galvanized drainpipe, I shall simply pick the one that I think would look best with white tie and tails.

AUGUST

I think I should feel considerably less rotten than I do this morning had I not learned all my anatomy from Arthur Mee's *Children's Encyclopaedia*. Never mind Ignatius Loyola, is my view: give a child to Arthur Mee until it is seven years old, and it will be his forever. Those early years are a voracious time for the burgeoning cerebrum, and a time, moreover, when information is most vividly embossed on its greedy little cells not by thinking but by imagination. The human mite, gobbling too fast to think, simply absorbs facts as pictures. Nor facts alone: trauma and taboo are likewise ineradicably imprinted, usually in a nano-second's flash, so never mind Sigmund Freud either, probably.

I recall my great colleague Bernard Levin once banging on hysterically about his arachnophobia, a thing so multi-rooted, it seemed, in ancient writ and demonology, sexual arcana, primitive iconography, prenatal sensation, neurasthenia, and all the rest, that even he could not find it in his huge brain to encompass or analyse all its miasmal sources – not while standing on a lavatory seat and screaming, anyway – but I rather fancy, given our co-membership of the Mee generation, that he in fact got his horror where I got mine. Under *Spider*, Mee offered a full-page colour plate of a thing like a crab in a ginger wig crunching its way through a hapless shrew. You could hear it swallow. After that, I could not look at even the closed volume without breaking

33

into a muck sweat.

Which, in my current febrility, neatly brings me to the image that has remained with me most vividly from those days, indeed has shaped my life: Mr Mee's transliteration of the human anatomy into visual terms comprehensible to the goggling tiny. Dropping an artist's cleaver through the body and unseaming it from the navel to the chaps, he revealed it to be nothing less than a Victorian factory, on the dozen sepia storeys of which hundreds of industrious little artisans in white overalls dug and stoked and stirred and dammed and sluiced and tinkered. In the skull, titchy telephonists toiled alongside minute photographers and electricians, in the cellars midget sweeps and sewermen cheerily went about the day's business in impressively spotless conditions, while on the bustling floors between, countless dedicated workers attended the boilers and turbines and crankshafts and pumps variously charged with transforming sprout and cutlet into energy. The text which went with this picture underlined Mee's – let us, for once, avoid the obvious and merely call it Granthamite – philosophy: 'Every part of your body is doing its bit for you, night and day; you have an obligation not to let it down. Work together!'

Manager sanum in corpore sano.

Since 1946 I have never been able to think of what hangs under my hat in any other way. I am the chief executive of a thriving enterprise zone, full of loyal little achievers. Despite four decades of sitting through biology lessons and television documentary alike, I do not see myself as complex chains of multicoloured plastic blobs, or teeming slides of a billion micro-organisms, or even the shimmering pink dispersal of Dewhurst's window. I am a big box of little men and we all look after one another.

Imagine then, my horror at waking, on Monday, with an inexplicable temperature of 103°, to be told by a doctor: 'You seem to have been treating your body rather badly. Run it down. I'll do some more tests, but I'm pretty certain that what you've contracted is glandular fever.'

You seem to have been treating your body rather badly. Did the man have any idea whereof he so nonchalantly spoke? This was not a simple question of neglecting diet or sleep, this was a moral question, this was about dereliction of duty: I, into whose charge the loyal and diligent workforce had been given, had grossly abused them. The factory was, dear God, *run down*! Images flashed up before me (put there, doubtless, by dog-tired, rubber-muscled, red-eyed little projectionists) of clapped-out gear, bent cams, rusted piping, stuck valves, flaking surfaces, seeping welds, with my desperately fatigued employees stumbling about, oil-streaked and aching, gamely struggling to keep their livelihood secure despite working conditions in flagrant contravention of every Factory Act pinned up beside my heart, that nucleus of the great powerhouse, in the days when it was as fresh and elastic as it came off Arthur's palate, a stranger to nicotine stain and cholesterol fur and the arrhythmic lurchings which now haunt its small hours and cause its elfin minders to glance up anxiously from their pools coupons.

Two days on, and lozenges of a dozen colours, shapes and sizes having been shovelled through by the trusty little navvies who stand sentinel at either tonsil, the factory is struggling to return to normal. One hopes only that the works can familiarize themselves with modern repair procedures. We are a traditional firm, hidebound even; we know where we are with Scott's Emulsion and J. Collis Browne. Do I, when the mild deliriums of the still watches come upon me, seem to hear far voices piping up, complaining of all these new-fangled things being too little and too late?

Or is that thrumming merely poor Arthur Mee, architect-philosopher of the grand design, spinning miserably in his grave?

I have chosen Georgian. I could have had Regency, I could have had Tudor, I could have had Farmhouse, but I have chosen Georgian. Indeed, had I not opted for off-the-peg and gone instead for something expensively bespoke, I could have had my own design, English Perpendicular, perhaps, with a couple of droll gargoyles and a flying buttress or two thrown in, possibly a Norman cat-flap, but since £935 + VAT seemed quite enough to pay for a garage door, I have chosen Georgian.

It is aluminium Georgian, of course: I could have had fibreglass for a lot less, but one should not sacrifice period authenticity to economy. If it's Georgian you're after, aluminium or nothing is my view.

They are out there now, fitting it. It is an up-and-over door, or will be when they have finished chopping holes in the house. I did not want an up-and-over aluminium door, mind, I liked our old pull-open wooden door, but when it became a pull-and-non-open door, I called them in and they said nobody has those any more, look at this catalogue, observe this infra-red technology, you do not even get out of your car, you drive through the beam and the door goes up and over electrically and you drive in, and it shuts automatically behind you.

I asked them how I got out of the garage.

They said I pushed a button in the wall and a portion of the door would open. It was, they assured me, foolproof.

I sometimes wonder if the manufacturers of foolproof items keep a fool or two on their payroll to test things. As a regular purchaser of goods so described, I have often toyed with the idea of bringing a case under the Trades Descriptions Act. If nothing else, it would be interesting to spectate the calling of expert witnesses:

'Mr Wisley, you are, I understand, a fool?'

'A leading fool, actually.'

'Just answer the question, yes or no.'

What bothers me even more than my own ineptitude, however, is that risk of breakdown, power cut, or any other of the thousand natural shocks that National Grid is heir to, which would leave me entombed. What would happen to that claustrophobia which discourages me from Tube travel, were I suddenly to be stuck in my own little carriage on the Necropolitan line?

I shall have to lay in a garage stock of tinned *foie gras*, bottled malt, and boxed Havanas. Which would at least give future Carters and Carnarvons something to think about when they finally broke through. Whatever else 20th-century Fool may or may not have believed, they would conclude, at least he thought he was in for a bit of a giggle on the other side.

The imminence of the door was also responsible, last Sunday, for triggering *frissons* of a different, though equally disturbing order.

My children being possessed of that teenage radicalism which leaves no bead undrawn when a bourgeois target seems to have poked its head above the parapet, they fell, at breakfast, on a chance remark by me that, if nothing else, the new door would be more secure than the old. Eyes rolled, shrieks flew: what was this if not further evidence of geriatric suburban paranoia? The Thing In The Suit, petrified lest unemployed left-wing drug-crazed Islamic soccer hooligans ran riot through his mortgage, aerosoling obscene holes in his ozone layer and leaving salmonella all over his books, was bunging up a portcullis.

Stung, I pointed out that I had not always lived the redbrick villa life, nor always touched my forelock for a monthly paycheck. Once, I had rented a tiny studio in Bohemia and chipped away at the unyielding rockface of the novel.

My daughter said, all right, then, Fyodor, let's go and have a look at it, I bet it wasn't a studio at all, I bet it was a studio *apartment*, in some ghastly jerry-built speculative development, I bet its bell chimed.

I parked at the bottom of Hampstead's Well Road, and together we strolled a route I had not strolled in a quarter-century, towards the Victorian yellow-brick wedge: Well Mount Studio, 20ft cubed, beneath a pitched glass north-lit roof, aproned by a triangular walled courtyard hardly larger than a folded tea-towel. But if you were twenty and bent on moving the world, you and your lever had somewhere to stand.

Fifty yards away, she suddenly stopped.

'Blimey!' she cried. 'They've put up a plaque!'

I peered, and it was true. It had not been there, then. Could such things be? *A. Coren, Wag, lived here?*

The truth was hardly less unsettling. *Mark Gertler, 1891-1939, Artist, lived here.* She asked who he was, and, as I told her, the memory of my entire tenancy ran under revision. Had Lytton Strachey stood sponging his gaunt footage in my sink? Had Dora

37

Carrington driven Gertler mad with her fraught virginity upon my sofa? Had Fry and Senhouse and Garnett and all the rest squeezed cheek by jowl in my moonlit courtyard, banging on about the shortcomings of the Bullnose Morris? What might Duncan Grant and Maynard Keynes have been up to in my curtained kitchenette?

And what might this haunted spot have made of me, had I never left?

My daughter was running down a different track. Youth is blunt.

'Funny,' she said, 'I can't see you here.'

'No up-and-over door?' I suggested.

'Something like that,' she said.

Taxi virumque cano. Cabbie number 14163, to be precise, who, as we lurched together down Horseferry Road last Friday, suddenly (triggered perhaps by a sudden shaft of sunlight) burst into *Oh What A Beautiful Morning*. I did not mind this at all. Though it doubtless infringes umpteen Carriage Office prohibitions, a yard or two of baritoned Hammerstein is immeasurably preferable to arguments in favour of drawing and quartering, detailed information concerning the exact weight of hay a Hackney carriage may carry on its roof, or invitations to guess who was sitting in that very seat only last night, not a stitch on under his trenchcoat and a foot shorter than he looks on the wossname, telly.

If, mind, this is the beginning of an admirable trend, may I suggest a more consonant repertoire? As one who has lolled happily in the gunwales while a gondolier not only punted through the engaging Venetian filth but trilled his native arias as he went, I see no reason why the London cabbie, as the tourist season burgeons, should not similarly leech his heritage for mutual gain. I have always felt sorry for foreigners cheated of the mufflered Cockneys they have been taught by Hollywood to expect: just think how their little faces would light up if their driver suddenly hurled back the partition and launched into *Any Old Iron* or *The Lambeth Walk*.

Steering one-handed, perhaps, in order to accompany himself on the spoons.

The oldest ex-parrot in England was what 14163 was carrying me to see. Pre-empting Monty Python by almost three centuries, it joined the choir invisible in 1702. It did so only three days after its illustrious mistress popped her clogs, but whether the bird threw in its mortal lot with hers from grief or because the way was now clear for an ill-wisher to strangle it, history does not say. History merely identifies it as a stuffed West African parrot, formerly the inseparable pet of Frances, Duchess of Richmond and Lennox.

You will find the pair of them still standing together in the crypt of Westminster Abbey. Well, to be strictly accurate, you will find the parrot standing next to a wax effigy of its mistress, since both taxidermy and good taste can go only so far: while the parrot is the real thing, the Duchess herself resides demurely encoffined in the Henry VII Chapel.

As she was the mistress not only of the parrot but also of Charles II, Frances is well worth narrow-eyed scrutiny. We are, after all, as close to her as Charles II ever got, vertically at least, and since her effigy was made before her death, we have to believe it is a good likeness or she would have had it turned into nightlights. It is at this point that the boggle enters the mind. For Frances is as plain as it is possible to be without requiring a licence to enter a public place. Furthermore, over and above the general homeliness, she has a specific physical feature so extraordinary that I am tempted to believe, on no evidence at all, that Charles, who could after all take his pick of the bunch, had a bizarre penchant for such curiosities.

Her beak is three times the size of the parrot's. It is like a scimitar. It leaves her considerable embonpoint in permanent shadow. It dominates the crypt. I have thought deeply about it since, and I have still not managed to work out how the king could have kissed her without having his cheek punctured. Indeed, the more one studies the Duchess's remarkable physiognomy, the more one is tempted to bizarre speculation concerning the amatory tastes of the Merry Monarch.

And the more one approaches the conclusion that the parrot

was almost certainly killed to keep its mouth shut.

While you're there – I'm assuming that the foregoing is irresistible – stroll to The Little Cloister for a somewhat more illuminating shaft on Restoration mortality. Set in the wall is a plaque commemorating the death of Mr Thomas Smith of Worcestershire *who through the Spotted Vaile of the Smal-Pox rendered a pure and unspotted soul to God, expecting but not fearing Death, which ended his Dayes March 10 Anno Dom 1663.* Despite the fact that Mr Smith was only 27 when the ghastly affliction carried him off, the times could clearly not allow any opportunity for wit to pass ungrabbed. While the spotted/unspotted pun is, I admit, fairly straightforward knockabout, the homonymous joke of *Vaile* is the work of a master.

I have bought a sphygmomanometer. You are the first people I have told, because I cannot pronounce it. My lips start to break up between syllables three and four. In order to buy it at all I had to point at it, mutely, in John Bell & Croyden, suppliers of medical ironmongery to the carriage trade, thereby incurring one of those herringbone glances woven from pity and derision which expert salespersons deploy against inexpert buypersons.

'Are you a doctor, sir?' he said.

Do you know the shop? It is in Wigmore Street, a gallstone's throw from Marylebone's – quite literal – fleshpots, and is in consequence packed with smug coves in three-piece worsted, truffling about for chic surgical gewgaws. Thus, when someone says, 'Are you a doctor, sir?' in a voice loud enough to be overheard, it is not unlike having someone say, 'Are you a member, sir?' when you are trying to sidle into the Athenaeum on the sly. People look up.

'Not entirely,' I replied. Under pressure, I tend, if not to crack, to buckle a bit. It was, I realised as soon as it hit the air, not the best answer, conjuring up as it did an image of someone about to park a battered caravan in Harley Street, nail a barber's pole to it, and begin stimulating phagocytes for spot cash.

'What I meant, sir, was do you want a professional instrument, or a home monitor?'

'I want to keep an eye on my blood pressure,' I said.

This time, I said it very quietly. Who could guess the lengths to which eavesdropping high-rent consultants might go when their bread-mouth ratio was threatened by DIY enthusiasts? They might not only have fallen on me and torn me limb from limb, they might also have sent in a huge bill for the professional service thus rendered.

It turns out to be a little cracker: fits the bicep as if bespoke, and emits a robust yet unhysterical bleep when reaching its systolic and diastolic poles. Also, a little red light goes on. It is astonishing what they can do for £49.95 these days.

All this started a week ago, when I disembarked from holiday feeling fit as a flea, and cannily hurtled round to the GP for my annual check-up before things could start going wrong and possibly require unsavoury new lozenges or expensive poking about. It was not, however, as smart a move as planned. My blood-pressure turned out to be unacceptably up. I could not account for this except by reflecting that one should wait more than 24 hours after paying any French hotel bill, to allow the blood to stop boiling.

Sternly enjoined to have an eye kept on the symptom, I agreed to a monthly examination; but as I walked home past the aforementioned chandlers, it suddenly occurred to me that I could do it myself and save £££s in my own home. So I do; up to twenty times a day.

What fun medicine is! What wonderful kit! Hats with lights on, precision pocket-mallets, shimmering Beano pliers, hand-turned/leather-trimmed optical gadgets against which no orifice can maintain its mystery, elegantly titchy electric saws, tiny anodised cubes in smart polished caskets . . . you can see how quacks become hooked, nothing to do with Hippocratic commitments to getting one's fellow man back on his feet in no time; it is all about toy trains.

O btainability is the time's plague. Engendered by the enterprise culture and exploited by the electronic one, obtainability is the curse which persuades people that they have to be in touch with one another at all times. It has become impossible to escape being got hold of.

Having resisted an answering machine, a carphone, a Telecom Gold mailbox, a personal pager, and all the other wondrous gubbins designed to keep me on inescapable call, I have finally been brought low by the humble Post-it. This is the yellow slip of paper on the gum for which the 3M Corporation spent millions of R & D dollars to ensure it would stick to everything else in the world, enabling urgent messages to be left for those who didn't want them.

They have taken over. I seem unable to go anywhere these days without finding a note stuck to something requiring me to take this or that action or phone this or that person. My family leave them on my shaving-mirror and bedside clock, my staff leave them on my typewriter and Anglepoise, friends and enemies leave them on my car windscreen and front gate, and yesterday new ground was broken when, stuck to my acacia tree, I found a message in garbled pidgin from our Neapolitan jobbing gardener demanding the provision of something which I have so far been unable to decipher.

Worst of all, I cannot now spot one of these horrors without feeling my heart go pit-a-pat. Can they, I wonder, be part of some huge plot engineered by John Bell & Croyden to seduce hypochondriacs?

SEPTEMBER

A novelist who shall be nameless – certainly if posterity has any sense – got so far up my nose on Monday that, respiratory physiology being the convoluted item it is, I now have to get him off my chest.

Some four weeks ago, I wrote him a brief business note. A fortnight later, I received in reply five pages of literary exotica so pretentiously florid that I had to spend half an hour dead-heading metaphors before I could determine what he was actually saying. What, though, stubbornly remained beyond determining was why quite so much time and energy should have been devoted to a thousand arcane polysyllables for which he was not being paid. That is not this fellow's way. Indeed, it is widely rumoured that, when approached by commissioning editors, he not only specifies his cost per word, he also enquires how many commas will be required, @ £3.95 a dozen.

This minor mystery was finally solved on Bank Holiday Monday, when I bumped into him in the ferris wheel queue on Hampstead Heath and was thus forced, willy-nilly, to compliment him upon his turgid epistolary dross. He nodded, smugly.

'The apple has changed my life,' he said.

It might have been Adam speaking, had he not gone on to explain that the Apple in question was his new word processor which automatically stored everything he wrote before printing it out. This meant he could now keep all his private

45

correspondence. Which in turn meant that it was not private correspondence any more, it was *The Collected Letters of Shalby Nameless*, composed and edited for hardback publication.

This is a bad business. If it catches on, nobody will write an honest letter ever again. Authors, particularly, will be unable to bang off a complaining bleat to their laundry without slipping in a paragraph on Negative Capability, a pithy shaft or two summing up contemporary mores, a feeble literary joke, a slug of scurrilous gossip, a note anent their *Work in Progress* for future biographers, and a couple of resonant quotes from Marcus Aurelius. Speaking as one who had rejoiced in the fact that the telephone had killed the art of letter-writing, I find the threat of its computer-enhanced return really rather horrible.

I have nothing else to report from Hampstead Heath Fair, except that there were eight ice-cream booths, none of which offered any flavour but crypto-vanilla. Nor do they use scoops any more – the stuff, which has the consistency of shaving foam, is extruded from the alloy rectum of a large hopper and, if there is a breeze, blows off your cone before you can get your tongue out.

Oh yes, and a gypsy lifted a fiver for telling me that I was either a barrister or a doctor with a scar on his knee. I rolled both trouser legs up, but she wouldn't give me my money back.

Our premises have become a GCSE clearing-house. We are the St Trinian's telephone exchange. Ever since the results were despatched last Thursday, hysterical teenage girls have been ringing up at all hours of the day and night to compare trauma with my daughter. Many of them call from those unpronounceable spots on the other side of the globe to which the middle classes have been driven in their search for original holidays to video, and, if Victoria is out, shriek their numbers at me so that she can call them back at little more than a quid a minute for an hour's commiseration.

At 3 am on Tuesday, I was booted from sleep by a child in Fiji, where it was 3 pm, but since she rang to sob that she had been given an E in Geography I felt uneasy about coming down too heavily on her ignorance of the time lag. She may well think that Cricklewood is a Solomon Island. I explained that I preferred not to wake my daughter, but when this was greeted from 12,000 miles away by the unmistakable noise of a tantrum being thrown with great force, I asked, albeit blearily, if I could help.

Did I, she faltered through the static, know anything about the rumour that the Geography GCSE exam had been an administrative cock-up, that there would be re-assessments, re-takes, drumhead courts martial of Kenneth Baker and Angela Rumbold, and so forth? I croaked that some kind of post mortem was supposed to be in the ministerial pipeline, soothed as best I could, and, mindful that a fellow-parent half a world away was footing a bill likely to put Fijian Telecom on an even keel for the rest of the century, rang off.

An odd business, all round. Given that its advertised purpose was to introduce a fairer, broader-based, less intensive and hence generally more relaxed form of assessment, GCSE seems to have plunged childhood back into the cut-throat days when education was about nothing more than success or failure. Furthermore, it has generated a national anxiety both in and for our children not seen since parents were required to hang gas-mask cases round their necks and wave them off to rural fosterhood.

Whom shall we blame? Do you know, I rather suspect that it could be something to do with the Prime Minister. Wait for a rash of spring books with titles like *Casualties of Achievement, The Meritocratic Downside*, and *The Age of the Swot*.

Whether we should attribute it to mere chance or to a hitherto unreported and somewhat unnerving element of the postal strike, I cannot say; but the only letter which managed to get through to me after the bar came down last week was from Bulgaria. Can there be Comintern moles within the Union of Communication Workers, burrowing through the mail mountains and bunging Giro-cheques and gas bills and writs and billets-doux into picket-guarded skips in order to destabilize and disrupt, but allowing egress to what might be urgent messages between international conspirators? There is no way of being sure, but it has ever been my rule of thumb, when national disorder threatens, to check whether there's a Balkan loitering on the 39th step.

The letter itself served only to confirm suspicions, though of what it was impossible to guess. Postmarked Gabrovo, it claimed to come from something called the House of Humour and Satire, which might have been anything from a sideshow at some Bulgarian Goose Fayre, offering bearded ladies and dancing fleas, to one of those emporia that sell sneezing powder and seebackascopes and buzzers which go off when you shake hands or, in this case perhaps, embrace a visiting trade mission.

Reading on, however, I learnt that the House of Humour and Satire claimed to be an academic institution 'devoted to the study of jokes', which was generously inviting me to Gabrovo to deliver a guest lecture on *The Role of Humour as a Political Weapon*. How simultaneously daft and poignant! Do these good folk still cleave to the fond belief not only that humour can be discussed at all, but also that jokes can make one whit of difference to the way the world is misruled? The role of humour is to make people fall down and writhe on the Axminster, and that is the top and bottom of it.

Or am I simply the intended victim − hence the unallayed suspicions − of a practical joke, cooked up by mischievous Bulgarians who are themselves falling about, at the thought of seducing vainglorious Western gullibles to Gabrovo, to be met at the airport by hoots, catcalls and sneezing powder?

If we were going to send anyone to Gabrovo, it surely ought to be Robert Morley. Not only would the sheer, well, Morleyness of him − that eye, that nose, that lip, that belly, that *presence* − confound any prankster, if prank it proved, and leave the broken Bulgarian japesters without a pogo stick to stand on (I have seen Morley sweep through an airport, and it might have been the old Queen Mary, boat or monarch, take your pick), but if the offer to speak proved genuine, I can think of no one better qualified to address the nature of comedy, just by standing up.

The guest of honour at the Foyle's Literary Lunch on Tuesday, by virtue both of being 80 and of having delivered, in *The*

Pleasures of Age, another fine fat book, the great man, shimmering in what was unquestionably the largest yellow suit ever built, turned in a long, extempore speech of such wit, risk, fun, timing and wicked charm as to leave his assembled co-professionals as helpless as Miss Foyle's paying punters.

I have nothing to say on the matter, except to count myself fortunate in being the beneficiary of timing, which meant that although there were three of my fellow *Times* diarists present with their snouts in the Dorchester trough, I am the one to whom it falls to wish Mr Morley a joyous and irrepressible continuation of his glorious boyhood.

Though I have never been able to remember whether Keats oded Autumn with twittering swallows gathering in the skies or gathering swallows twittering in the skies (you can, incidentally, become unhinged by trying to decide whether it matters which), I have always suffered acute pangs at other tell-tale signs of summer's lease being foreclosed. It is possibly something to do with being mortal, but whatever it is that sharpens the September senses, it was honing flat out last weekend.

A glimmer of afternoon sunshine having enticed me to the playing-fields across the road, I found in progress a cricket match so plangent with time's resonances as to make the eyes prick, fill and swim – had swallows decided to gather in the skies, I should have had to rely on the twittering alone to draw my attention to the fact. Two elderly teams were flailing gamely at one another in what was not only the last match of the season but might very well, from the look of it, have been the last match of their careers – it would have taken an orthopaedic experience far beyond my own to distinguish confidently between the snick of bat and the click of joint.

And then, with the actual and the metaphorical gloamings fusing for the final over, the groundsman's tractor rolled up to the boundary with its drear winter load; and, as the old men clapped one another in from the darkling field, they were passed by the groundsman's tactlessly youthful henchboys carrying out rugger posts. Which, even as the old men's studs were clattering on the pavilion steps, they began to put up on the suddenly former cricket field.

What with death moaning and singing on our boulevards as diplomats, soldiers, villains and crackpots express their views in lead, I felt it no bad time to drop into my local nick to ascertain how the current firearms amnesty was coming along. According to the newspapers, the national picture was all very cheering, with howitzers and doodle-bugs and old torpedo-boats piling up so encouragingly that it might very soon be safe to start taking the dog out again. What, then, of North London?

Yes, said the duty sergeant at West Hampstead Police Station, we have had a Response. What kind of Response, I inquired? We have had six cartridges handed in, said the sergeant.

The point is, should I take this to be a soothing indication of local innocence, or exactly the opposite?

Call it the enterprise culture, call it old-fashioned luck, but it is not every day that a humble suburban lavatory gets the chance to become spokesman for a major building society.

Not that I was, all things considered, a bad lavatory. A shade ribald, perhaps, but fundamentally worthy. All in all, a decent sort of bog. The year was 1980, and though mine was by no stretch of the ear a household voice, it had, by dint of a little facetious broadcasting, come to the attention of a small advertising agency charged with offloading a new aerosol germicide onto a general public it had persuaded to fret about porcelain susceptibility.

The agency, its letter explained, had shot a 30-second animated cartoon starring an anthropoid privy, and was looking for someone to speak its lines. So, lured by the familiar rumours – I was also, at that time, writing a series for Leonard Rossiter, who rarely ignored an opportunity to point out that he was getting 50 times as much for chucking Cinzano over Joan Collins as he was for spouting my tripe – I hurried to a cellar in Broadwick Street, where the agency projected the cartoon on to the wall of my recording booth. The lavatory's lid and seat went up and down, amusingly liplike, and I had to keep repeating, synchronously, 'What a difference a spray makes!' until man and latrine were as one. I also had to chortle a bit, as only lavatories can.

They gave me £200, which Rossiter said was the smallest amount ever earned in a Soho afternoon by anyone. The ad never went out. I stayed by the telephone for a year or two, but when the news broke that Stallone had decided to cast himself as Rocky, I finally chucked in the thespian sponge.

And then, last Thursday, eight years on, another call came, this time from a very swell agency indeed. Abbott Mead Vickers wished to know whether I was available to embody nothing less than the corporate identity of a building society so leading that half the country is in hock to it. Why me, I wondered? Had they seen my chuckling dunny? Was it a byword still, wherever creative departments foregathered? AMV demurred: just heave to off Soho Square tomorrow afternoon, was the message, and let the chips fall where they may.

A booth again, a little film, a headphone, a mike. But this time, no jocund plumbing was required, rather the firm smack of executive gravitas. I was, I think, rather good. A bit like Trevor Howard. I would have taken out a mortgage with me like a shot, or, alternatively, have emptied my own jingling sock into that corporate coffer.

Yesterday, AMV sent me a little note and a couple of consolatory bottles. Pretty good bottles, but you'd get change out of £200. I seem to have gone downhill a bit since my heyday.

L ot 1, ladies and gentlemen, a vintage automaton, offered as seen, and described as dilapidated, foxed, and considerably distressed. The object – which appears to date from about the middle of the last century but is in fact of marginally more recent manufacture – is of rude design, common shape, and undistinguished aspect, superficially cleaned but otherwise unrestored, most moving parts being in poor working order. Its mechanism starts with a push, whereafter the object will move about in a jerky fashion before falling over. It has been crudely decorated to resemble a cricketer, though not closely.

Quite why I should have been hobbling out to bat last Saturday in the annual Antique Dealers Cricket Match is difficult to explain without impugning the honour of that great trade. Let us just say that it is in the nature of the beast to go in for, er, flexible labelling, which allows them to describe me as an antique dealer on the grounds that one or either of them has, over the years, been able to offload junk on me for folding money.

I thus qualify as willow-fodder, which means that every September I am compelled to take guard on a steep incline above Stow-on-the-Wold and wait for some sturdy young huckster to materialize out of the sleet and kill me.

This, mind, would happen only by accident – in my unique case. Because this is no ordinary friendly. For every other day of the year, these fellows are at one another's commercial throats; and since this is a fixture traditionally preceded by a great deal of expensive lubricant, the match is played in a mood of retributive venomousness so drunkenly erratic as to keep casualty departments from Oxford to Cheltenham on the *qui vive* throughout the long day.

Being a mere customer, however, I have always been exempt from the professional score-settling. Thus, while it was no surprise to me, walking in at number five, to have the departing batsman mutter as he passed me his gloves that he had been run out by his partner as the result of his having stitched him up over a dubious break-front bookcase at the Olympia Antiques Fair, I could feel confident that of all the risks I was about to run, this was not of their number.

I had elegantly snicked my way to seven and was prudently allowing a full toss to float past the off stump, when the wicketkeeper suddenly whipped off the bails. Since my back foot was safely planted, I grinned at the umpire, a hitherto jolly chandler in, as I recall, Jacobean oak.

'Goodbye,' said the umpire.

In the pavilion, my captain was broaching an umpteenth crate. 'Did you see that?' I cried. 'What's got into the bloody umpire?'

The captain eased a cork. 'I understand you've never bought anything from him,' he said.

Funny game, cricket.

Yesterday morning, driving to Patrick Lichfield's chic Portobello hangar for a publicity snap, and thus desperately attempting to think cheery thoughts in order to put a smile on a face which habitually photographs as Kafka's glummer brother, I passed, as ill-luck would have it, one of the bleakest sights I have ever seen.

In the middle of Chamberlayne Road, Kensal Rise – itself a spot instinct with Victorian gloom – stands a derelict redbrick island. It seems to serve no function but to display a spotty iron sign which mystifyingly reads: FEEDING THE PIGEONS IS PROHIBITED. Beneath this dispiriting legend, half a dozen drizzleswept and generally seedy birds waited motionless, like old men hanging about on a discontinued branch-line platform. Why it should be legally forbidden to feed them, why they should continue to assemble there in pointless hope of tucker, are questions it is impossible to address. But they will unquestionably surface in my photograph.

Patrick, not unreasonably chastened by my lack of chirpiness, posed me holding a rolled-up copy of *The Listener* to my ear (geddit)?, but the thing in his viewfinder was clearly more *Pagliacci* than clown.

He thought for a bit. 'Say money,' he said, at last.

'Why?'

'Money makes people laugh,' said Patrick. 'Don't ask me why.'

'Money,' I said.

Patrick thought for another bit. 'Say porridge,' he said.

Ten minutes ago, stumped for a succinct concluding paragraph which would resonate in your heads after I had gone, I sighed, quitted my unyielding typewriter, and walked across Old Marylebone Road for a cup of coffee. It was as I was tearing the corner from the sugar sachet that I noticed the bright blue legend on its flank. It said: *Whitworth's Quick-Dissolving Granulated Sugar.*

What boons technology toils at, even as we sleep! For years we have all been somehow struggling along with ordinarily-disolving granulated sugar, totally unaware that shedsful of eminent scientists were engaged in taking the age-old challenge by the throat. And at last, like Edison before them, like Curie, like Fleming, like Watson and Crick, they have cracked it.

My only problem now is what to do with all the valuable time I shall henceforth be saving.

OCTOBER

On Monday, as literary coincidence would have it, the fog rolled about Norfolk with fog's habitual inconsistency, unsettled and – given my mission – unsettling. I drove the A11 as in an aeroplane negotiating cloud: there would be wet walls of the stuff, then floating disconnected lumps, then sudden dazzling lacunae, sun above and a thick white sea beneath, full of legless cows bobbing about like inflatable swimming toys. Rare human strollers loomed, and stared, and vanished. Just the day for prisons. Magwitch was out there somewhere, looking for livers.

Wayland Prison lies in the fenny featurelessness between Thetford and Watton, though you would be pushed to spot it as such. Coyness requires the smallest signpost to read H.M.P. Wayland, as if it were some shore-based training establishment full of midshipmen practising semaphore. Not that appearances altogether gainsay that guess. Wayland is a mere three years old and architecturally a product of the New Municipalism: at first sight, the low redbrick blocks could be a comprehensive school run by an enlightened Tory administration whose first progressive act had been to bung a 17-foot-high steel mesh fence around it. As it were, H.M.C. Boyson. But if, as you approach the gate, you cock an ear, you know this could never be a school. Wayland is silent. There are 480 detainees, and you do not hear a sound. In fog, it is unquestionably eerie.

The fog irritates everyone. The prisoners cannot go out on working parties because of the risk of their staying out. Thus, routine is upset, and prisons run on routine. Fortunately, the fog is not thick enough to obscure the fence, because that might disturb the routine even more. How, you might ask if you were as naïve as I, does a man scale a flexible 17 foot fence? The answer is that we do not know the next method. We know only the last method. The last method, a few weeks back, was to take a seeming-innocent table-tennis net, twist it into a hawser and bung one end at the fence so that the support-clip grappelled the top. Send us a postcard when you get to Switzerland, Skipper!

A prison officer mutters: 'Everything in here is a key. You can see them looking at everything – a spoon, a bar of soap, a jar of bloody marmalade – and trying to work out how they can use it.' Beneath this growl, as in almost any observation officers make about prisoners, an irritable respect lurks. It is a respect for cunning. Cunning is not much prized outside, because to be really effective cunning requires conspiracy, and, ironically, confinement is the friend of conspiracy. The result, in terms of the social environment, is most peculiar: to the civilian, the atmosphere is one of total and permanent suspicion. Everybody watches everybody else all the time. I inquire as to whether all this hard eye-contact makes the officers feel uncomfortable, and learn, of course, that they get a lot more uncomfortable when it suddenly stops.

My invitation to Wayland was generated some weeks ago in my *Times* column by an incautiously flip remark concerning the number of men to a slops-bucket, whereafter I was quite properly asked to come and see for myself. But how properly is properly? The invitation was couched in a letter so shimmeringly stylish, so joyously witty, and so adroitly interlarded with arcane references to Congreve, Himmler, Mussulman cuisine and our own dear Bernard Levin, that the eagerness with which I accepted it had less to do with a hunger to inspect the plumbing than with a curiosity to find out why the signatory had chosen to be a prison officer rather than take a crack at the Booker.

But when we met at the gate and I congratulated him, he confessed he had not written it, merely, such are Her Majesty's regulations, signed it. The invitation had been composed by a prisoner – not inappropriately, one currently being entertained for fraud. Like Cyrano, he had wooed me under cosmetic cover; like Roxanne's, my flinty heart wilted at the poignancy, even as the prisoner and I cackled over the daftness of it all. I met him in the chapel – he is also two dab hands at the piano – where he was accompanying a young violinist, and I could not forbear from wondering what they were both doing inside. Several years, was the short answer.

It would be improper to call it waste, but in a world woefully short of creative talent, it is disturbing to read the words, hear the music, see the paintings, handle the sculptures of Wayland's talented inmates, and to ponder the use of the experience as a matrix for the world beyond the fence. Can it be that criminals are more creative than their respectable peers? Or is it rather that creativity would express itself more generously if only the rest of us were, as one might say, given time to explore it?

The day-tripper should take care. The food is good, the cells are singles, the beds are clean, and the buckets have indeed been replaced by individual flushers. Those of us who have promised themselves for thirty years that they would get down to the novel if only they could find a bit of breathing-space might well find themselves wondering if the table-tennis stunt works from the outside in.

There are some seventy of them here, on this chill Saturday night, and they are called Ragtag and Albipedius and Scorpio and Doghouse and Nibor and Blod, but they look normal enough. Indeed, given that they are the cleverest people in the world, the fact that they appear so normal – greeting, chortling, sipping, nibbling – is perhaps the most unsettling element of the whole affair. Especially as they have chosen to forgather on the fourth floor of the Drury Lane Moat House, one of those Legoland hotels in which men who look not unlike those currently present convene to celebrate record annual sales of chipboard shelving and cut-price alarm systems and rexinette calculator cosies.

Some of these, of course, may do just that, when they are not carrying out the arcane duties which attach to being Salamanca, or Gong, or Eel. For they have other lives, somewhere, under normal names, at normal desks and workbenches, going home, doubtless, to normal mates in normal houses. Though you would not guess so tonight: tonight, the outsider feels himself to have walked into the wonky world of Greene and Chesterton and Buchan. This is the Club of Queer Trades, whose members chat in riddles and laugh in code.

For this is the annual dinner of those who set *The Listener* Crossword, that infamous weekly cerebrocide which leaves Nobel laureates bouncing off the rubber walls of sanatoria, and drives Senior Wranglers to plunge terminally into the Cam. One glance tells you why *agon* fathered *agony*. And since I professionally bestride the world's two most famous crosswords, as editor there and columnist here, you will appreciate my mixed feelings upon learning, over the kipper paté, that my Saturday neighbour, Phi, does *The Times* crossword in under four minutes.

Esoteric rages boil. A recent puzzle, lunatically complicated by a rubric explaining that every word in it was a misprint, is roundly attacked by some sadist complaining that the misprints were not unfathomable enough. Another agitated buff wants me to run crosswords in colour, so that a further dimension of incomprehensibility may be stirred in. The hue clue. A third addict explains that reading has become difficult, since even a bedtime chapter of *Winnie the Pooh* presents him with a hundred anagrams, and murders sleep.

How strange it is, to have this intellectual firepower in notional thrall. These could be my Tontons Macoutes, my Green Berets, my SAS! If only I could combine and channel these extraordinary ratiocinative forces, what might I not . . . Fortunately for world equilibrium, they are immeasurably smarter than I am. All they want to do is cobble crosswords together.

I wonder, though, what they – for all their brilliance – would have answered had I asked them about lead-free petrol? As a man attempting to raise both children and trees, I grow increasingly irritable about the insouciance with which bright, influential, and otherwise concerned folk refuse to inform themselves about the muck which is rotting brains and foliage alike, and which may be easily and cheaply reduced.

On Sunday, we played lunchtime hosts to friends for whom the foregoing qualifications are the barest blueprint of decency. They are not only good and worthy people, they also carry clout. The group contained one of our wiser MPs, a national newspaper editor, three responsible journalists, a couple of honourable lawyers, the managing director of a large company, and four senior doctors. Beyond the windows, the acid rain was scything into the garden, and, nudged by a stray remark about a venerable acacia tree I have which is going down with 100-octane scrofula, the talk turned to lead-free petrol. Everyone had a lot to say, not all of it uncynical, about the recent greening of Mrs Thatcher, until, on a suspicious whim, I asked them about their own cars.

Not only did none of them drive on lead-free petrol, not a single soul even knew whether their car was capable of doing so, nor had made any inquiry about the cheap and simple job of converting it if it wasn't. Shocking, really: when there is so little one is able personally to do about holes in the ozone layer, or the destabilizing expunction of the rain forests, or the ghastly fouling of the oceans, you would think, would you not, that the rare opportunity actually to bring some benefit to the poor old environment – and the children doomed to inherit it – would be eagerly grasped?

Sorry for the rhetoric. Just trying to clear the air.

I do not, however, apologise for the dandiness of 'You would think, would you not.' You should not need to be a *Listener* cryptologist to spot it as a tribute to Russell Harty, from whose memorial service I have just returned, and the echo of whose unforgettable locutions resonated through St James's, Piccadilly, with that special poignancy lost voices have.

It was a fine, apt, ringing celebration, a concatenation of Blackburn and Hollywood, *Broadway Babes* and *The Biggest Aspidistra in the World* sung in harness, heartfelt and brainthought addresses delivered by Ned Sherrin and John Birt and Sue Lawley and Penelope Keith and Alan Bennett, and underneath the everlasting arms. But at the end of it all, the voice that lingered in the memory was the one we hadn't heard.

Odd, to be holidaying in a spot where the souvenir industry is based entirely upon liver. Generally a souvenir is a tiny building for keeping cigarettes in. A Taj Mahal, an Alpine chalet, an Arc de Triomphe, a Sydney Opera House. In the more breakable versions, you lift the roof and the tiny building plays'O Mine Papa' or 'Waltzing Matilda'. Alternatively, it is a tiny man for keeping cigarettes in. Shakespeare, Mozart, Plato, a beefeater, a sumo wrestler, Sir Harry Lauder. If it comes from Brussels, un-speakable possibilities attach, quite literally, to the tiny man's accommodation of the cigarettes.

In the Périgord, however, the souvenirs are produced exclusively by geese. Every other shop window is stacked to the gunwales with elaborately constructed displays of *foie gras*. You may buy it tinned or boxed or jarred, fresh or half-cooked or cooked; you may buy it *en bloc*, or as *terrine*, or as *paté*; you may buy it in an infinite variety of truffled elaborations; you may buy examples which have won gold medals at myriad *Foires de Foie*, or examples endorsed on the tin by talking geese. There are, as with wine, *grands marques* and *petits*; you may choose assembly-line produce or recherché little numbers lovingly hand-swollen by one man working in one hut, possibly only on one goose.

It is quite impossible to choose: mobs of bemused tourists amble hopelessly from shop to shop in the vain attempt to assess this offering against that. If you invite the opinions of staff or local *habitants*, acrimonious debates ensue as to relative merits, and you have to creep quietly away while the disputant gourmets are hurling arcane liver opinions at one another, and seek sanctuary in the shop across the street. Where it starts all over again.

The sheer spectacle of the towering piles conjures unanswerable questions. At a median £20 for a 200-gramme tin, how do these shops carry such immense stock? In Sarlat, while the patron was excitedly button-holing my wife on the virtue of glazing a *bloc* with a half-glass of warmed Montbazillac on the night prior to serving, I ran a test-count which revealed that this somewhat seedy little establishment was sitting on around

£40,000 worth of poultry-gland.

Yet more imponderable, given that Sarlat alone offers about two dozen shops and is itself but one town among many, where are all the geese? The averagely bloated goose-liver weighs 800 grammes, or four small tins. Scribbling rapidly on the back of a postcard, I calculated that Sarlat alone – just on what was being displayed, disregarding what they had in the basement – was offering the potted remains of some 20,000 birds. Where, then, were the living geese? The most conservative extrapolation suggested that the Périgord probably contained a million of them. The countryside should have been packed beak to beak, the roads blocked with waddling processions, probably standing on one another's shoulders.

In four days, we saw 11. This period included a night at a hilltop château outside Cahors which has a telescope for scanning a horizon 12 miles distant. Ten days on, my right eye still waters from a scrutiny which produced not a single goose. Furthermore, the dawns were silent. I'd thought geese cackled; I'd heard they hissed. But from a million beaks, nary a sound.

We bought half a dozen assorted tins of the stuff. Empty, they will be ideal for keeping cigarettes in.

An unanticipated pleasure on the trip was basking in the Gallic esteem in which our radiant leader is held, especially in the aftermath of the notorious Bruges speech, like the *Figaro* leader which clarioned *Encore un triomphe pour La Dame de Fer!* I had never guessed at the reverence with which the ordinary Frenchman pronounces her very name. They even go to atypically xenophiliac lengths to get their tongues into the unaccustomed interdental position, to avoid ending up with 'Satcher'. I could not recall anything like it since the days when Frenchmen would rush up to me in the street, shake my hand, and cry 'Bobby Sharltoon!'

The esteem, mind, is not political. It is the adulation of stardom, virtually irrespective of principle or action. Mrs Thatcher is, *tout simple*, the most famous woman in the world, and there is no question but that a little of the awe with which the French regard this tabloid achievement rubs off, willy-nilly, on the visiting Briton. It has not been thus for some time, possibly since Churchill, and I have to say that it is not unpleasing – whatever guilts, for whatever reasons, may go with one's simpering acquiescence in their plaudits.

Hurtling homeward on the N19, we spotted a signpost to Colombey-les-deux-Eglises, allowed curiosity a brief detour, and, in the shadow of the enormous memorial Cross of Lorraine which commands the landscape in metaphorical echo of that earlier dominance, fell into conversation with a Frenchman who, within three sentences, was bracketing de Gaulle and Thatcher as visionary giants.

Does there spring to mind a commemorative symbol which, one day, we should erect on a green hill without the city wall of Grantham? It has not yet sprung to mine, but if you can come up with one which fits posterity's bill, there's a tin of *foie gras* in it for the winner.

NOVEMBER

Were you seeking to pinpoint the subtle differences between Proust's sensibilities and my own, you would need look no further than Mare Street, E8. Where Marcel required only the delicate collision between incisor and dunked madeleine to exhume buried infancy, mine sprang out like a ferreted rabbit at the first acrid whiff of the Hackney Empire's proscenial dust.

Given that the main constituent of domestic grime is, I understand, old desquamated skin, and that the stage of the Hackney Empire appears to have gone unswept for half a century, I could well, last Saturday, have been sniffing pure Max Miller; if not, indeed, Little Tich and Marie Lloyd. But whatever it was, its familiarity detonated the memory: the instant I set toe on stage I was suddenly back in the Forties, to that terrible moment in *Cinderella* when Tommy Trinder demanded that every tot in the house step up and help him sing his song, and my mother – normally the most sensitive of women – grasped the scruff of my neck and, swept along no doubt by the communal tide of maternal ambition, thrust me forward to embark on that glittering theatrical career which was to last a full five minutes before collapsing in hysterical tears. Even now, I am unable to sit in the stalls without breaking out in a muck sweat lest Hamlet suddenly invite me to come up and help him finish off Claudius.

Last Saturday the stage was empty but the view was the same:

four tiers of serried plush and gilded plaster rolling back as many decades and refilling the ears with vanished cackling. I was there not, this time, to wave my handkerchief when Buttons cried *Puff, puff, choo, choo, and off we go*! but to chuck a bit in the box to help preserve the only Edwardian variety palace to strike the bingo shackles from its feet and be reborn free. Nine years ago, as Mecca began dismantling the old dear, English Heritage came to the aid of a distraught Hackney Society and, after a brief court skirmish, a deal was struck with the Hackney Empire Preservation Trust, to whom Mecca would sell the building on the undertaking that the Trust would restore it.

Much of the restoration has been carried out, the theatre has been up and running variety for a year – the foyer sports handbills for George 'I'm Not Well' Williams and Syd Wright Ace Xylophonist and, oh joy!, Billy Moore the Yodelling Accordionist – but Mecca Leisure still requires £150,000 for the freehold if the place is not to revert to bouncing ping-pong balls and short-term dreams.

Help buy it. Phone Ann Cartwright on 986-0171. It's the only remaining purpose-built variety theatre in the south, and it must not be purpose-unbuilt. Remember Max Miller's immortal words? '*There'll never be another*!'

I would seem to have got up the nose of Malawi's Minister of Justice. Nor does the Minister of External Affairs have a good word to say about me. As for the Minister of Works and Supplies, he is at one with the Minister of Agriculture in believing me to be a thoroughly bad lot.

Since all these influential fellows are not only one and the same man but also reside in happy co-existence beneath the natty suiting of the President For Life, you will understand my concern at having fallen so foul of Dr Hastings Kamuzu Banda that he will not have me in the house. Or, at any rate, my books.

This dispiriting intelligence arrived via Paul Theroux, a fellow victim of Dr Banda's displeasure, who was kind enough to send me a photostat of Malawi's *Catalogue of Banned Publications*, which normally costs, I note, 3 *kwasha*. I do not know how much 3 *kwasha* is, since the *kwasha* – or, when singular, possible *kwashum* – has never appeared on those annual royalty statements which mark the beginning and end of my interest in foreign exchange rates; but however much it is, I am grateful to Mr Theroux for saving me from forking it out. If Hastings Banda won't buy my books, I don't see why I should buy his.

What baffles me is why he won't. The *Catalogue* does not say. It merely places my name between Coral, K., author of *Lesbo Nurses On The Make*, and Cox, Alain, author of *The French Maid* – and thus not to be confused with Cox, Richard (*Blow me Hot, Blow Me Cool*), Cox, William (*Hot Times*), or Cox, M. (*Oversexed Astronauts*).

Fascinated to discover how my unsalacious cobblings might have placed me in the somewhat single-minded company of these other toilers in the literary vineyard, I embarked on a series of intercontinental phone calls costing God knows how many *kwasha*, none of which shed the faintest glimmer, especially the final desperate one to the Government Printer in Zomba, identified as the office responsible for publishing the pamphlet, who listened, laughed, and rang off.

At least, he *said* he was the Government Printer. More likely Hastings Banda again.

If only the good doctor had the funnybone of the young black dude whose boy racer turboed past me yesterday on Finchley Road! As the quadri-barrelled exhaust dwindled, its plumes framed a number plate that made the spirits somersault: IAGO.

Othello is avenged.

Like most far-sighted citizens, I was immensely cheered by the broadcasting White Paper. Or, rather, by its implications. When it comes to White Papers, as you will have noticed, it is always the implications on to which pundits latch. This is generally because the explications are (a) incomprehensible, and (b) not worth a light, anyhow: all we need ever concern ourselves with is What Does This Mean For The Future?

What the White Paper means for my future is that any day now

I shall almost certainly have my own television station. Network, even. I have read Mr Hurd's catchy tract with an assiduity which has left my eyes rolling around my head like marbles in a saucer, and it is quite clear to me that, provided I do not allow anything into the Rees-Mogg living-room which might frighten the horses, I am free to set up in the entertainment business as soon as my satellite is launched and spinning. I need make no franchise bid, register no company, leave no token of good faith or solvency with the Home Office or the DTI. I do not even have to take Mr Hurd out for a large one. All I need do is wave Section 6, para 31: 'The Government proposes to leave the further development of other satellite services to the market'.

It will perhaps be queried whether I can get into that market, given that the base figure for a satellite-cobbling, as of my Tuesday ring-round, was some £20 million, a figure likely to make my bank manager look out of the window and pull his ear-lobe, if past requests to tide me over till Friday are anything to go by. But that was Tuesday; many of you will have had those conversations in Dixons where a salesman points out that, ten years ago, the calculator in your hand would have been the size of St Paul's, and I have every confidence that within a very short time satellites will be £6.99, to include free launch.

My programmes will cost nothing. I was much cheered to hear the ululations rising over Hampstead Heath and Camden Hill on Monday over the imminent *Qualitätsdämmerung*, as smarties kept chanting that this was the end of *Jewel in the Crown* and *Brideshead Revisited*, which seemed to be the only two examples they could think of. For my money (which it is) I have had quite enough of quality drama: I see no reason for interpreting *Brideshead Revisited* at £500,000 an hour when you can not only buy the original for £3.95 but also enjoy it in the bath without risk of electrocution.

Thousands of extremely cheap programmes are exactly what we need, rather than a couple of annual blockbusters for which jumboloads of stellar salaries have been set down in Death Valley in order to fabricate, inadequately, an Abyssinia which Evelyn Waugh could reproduce in two sentences. My satellite will beam such low-budget screen gems as *Three Hundred Holiday Slides* (a visual treat with the added bonus, for my balance sheet, of forming the basis of my peak-time quiz show, *Guess Whose Head?*) and if anyone wants the classics, then I shall read them aloud from my Cricklewood *fauteuil,* a jar of inexpensive daisies behind me and a bottle to hand of some single malt whose distiller will be happy to cough up a subventional bob or two for the opportunity of commending his product to a select group of the discerning.

You do not need a star for that. I leave it to my flusher competitors to assault my rating with *Bob's Bleak House.*

With my low-budget satellite, of course, I shall not be required to sign up a royal heir to present a controversial documentary.

My own *Vision of Britain* will be shot from my office window. Even as I type, I can see a cheery group of decolleté buttocks refurbishing my local, at the corner of Marylebone's Homer Street. It used to be called The Olive Branch and was much loved for that brown seediness which is an integral part of our drinking heritage. Now it is being not only designer-tarted, but re-christened The Quintin Hogg. The great man himself is coming down on November 21 to open it. This depresses me enormously: I do not want, of a lunchtime, to pop into The Quintin Hogg for a quiche and Badoit. Where will it end? Are we soon to have The Dog and Tebbit, or The Two Jolly Kinnocks? Are sign-painters even now cackling over their preliminary sketches for The Parkinson's Arms?

It may be that I should, on Wednesday, have empathized less with Kenneth Baker had I not been doing so at 21 Craven Hill, Bayswater. This is not to say, mind, that I have not always had something of a soft spot for the Education Secretary: a politician who has produced a book of poems entitled *I Have No Gun But I Can Spit* may be forgiven much – even the fact that he once taught gunnery to the Libyan army, when teaching them to spit might have been not only privately more consistent, but also globally more sensible.

Now, Craven Hill is the northern slope of Notting Hill, and I arrived at Number 21 of the former via the stone's throw which separates it from Number 45 of the latter, this being my shortest route home from the National Curriculum Council, whither I had gone to collect the just-published *English for Ages 5 to 11*, the spunky little pamphlet commissioned by Mr Baker's department.

As I strolled down Craven Hill, I noticed a rocking horse atop a pole, because this is the kind of thing you do notice, especially if the rocking horse is looking down on a full-size Regency locomotive. I crossed the road, to discover that these two engaging items stood sentinel to The London Toy Museum. Since I had never visited it, since it offered a coffee-shop, and since there could hardly be a fitter place to read a treatise on 5-11 education, I gave serendipity its head, and went in.

The coffee shop turned out to have the best view from its windows of any coffee shop I had hitherto seen. It looks out over a lake, and beside the lake runs a railway; but this landscape would be clearable in a single bound, if you had a bit of a run at it, because it is a scale model. Beyond the rim of your cup, yesteryear's steam trains chug by, and even as they prick adult nostalgia for the real thing, so they reactivate infancy's greed for the wondrous miniatures themselves. You cannot have either, any more, says the view.

When I finally managed to drop my blurring eyes to *English for Ages 5-11* it turned out not to be too bad, as pamphlets go, despite itself giving hospitality to too many sentences which only a bureaucrat would identify as English. But it was supportive of standards for the written language to which those who care about it could take little exception, and its plans for achieving those standards seemed wise and practical enough.

It was only when it addressed the pricklier topic of spoken English that it chickened unforgivably out. 'It is,' murmured the pamphlet, 'unrealistic to require children to speak Standard English in the classroom if it is not their native dialect,' a view with which I would not disagree, did the pamphleteers not go on to explain that non-standard English embraced such uses as 'we was; he ain't done it; she come here yesterday; they never saw nobody'.

This is not non-standard English. It is standard non-English, and I cannot see how a child can be taught to appreciate what comes off the page if he is that insensitive to what comes off the tongue. Since this was the recommendation which, I gathered, most disturbed Mr Baker, it will now be seen why heart cleft to heart last Wednesday, and how the Toy Museum fitted in: for the place is about the way childhood things once were, and he and I received short shrift from non-standard English, then. In wet weather, my ear still smarts.

Not that there isn't a curious conundrum which requires solving if we are to take this matter seriously: why does a particular charm attach to kids who don't talk proper? The Toy Museum was packed to the gunwales with riotous school parties, and as I finished the pamphlet and began my tour, I came around a corner to have my knees collided with by two tiny shriekers. They recovered, and looked up. 'Sorry,' said one, 'me and him was looking for the wossname.'

As a piece of communication, it was a mite short on clues, but it had, I don't know, a kind of poetry. It went with their rolled-down socks and unkempt nostrils and – well, you had to be there. I should like them to get the bits sorted out before they hit man's estate, but there is no gainsaying the appeal of a tot's gamey demotic. Why should this be?

A further question, prompted by the fact that beneath the cheery cacophony, the most noticeable noise at the Toy Museum is rhythmic background thudding. It is the sound of tiny foreheads banging against display cases in a desperate bid to get closer to the fire-engine and fort. Why do children take so long to comprehend plate-glass? My own spent several years in Elastoplast before outgrowing not the habit, but museums. I don't understand this. Even a bumblebee eventually twigs.

Shall I recommend the Toy Museum? It's a magical spot, but you have to be a brave big soldier if you are not to wallow uncontrollably before Meccano windmills and balsa Blenheims and Dinky vans with signs on them for Virol and Germolene, and umpteen buses with passengers painted in their windows who gaze imperishably at you in the enchanting Tin Toy Room.

And what a delightful name *that* is! I have noted it down, in case I am ever called upon to christen a Burmese.

Though loath as any other hack to circumscribe my trawl, I nevertheless feel it would be unfair not to point out that most of today's musings will be of interest only to readers keen on touring Mars by balloon. Even Professor Carl Sagan, who has urged me to pass his thrilling invitation on, would not, I'm sure, wish to fritter the valuable time of those who prefer to think of stars as something to look up at, rather than down from.

The professor wrote to me from Pasadena on Monday, in his awesome capacity as President of the Planetary Society. '*Dear Fellow Citizen of the Planet Earth,*' he began – a refreshing change, I might say, from the vocative style of my other Monday correspondents, North Thames Gas and HM Customs and Excise, in whom a little cordial fraternity would not come amiss – '*the Planetary Society is dedicated to the exploration of the solar system by spacecraft, and the quest for extraterrestrial life and intelligence. Please take a few moments to read the enclosed letter from our Executive Director, Dr Louis Friedman.*'

How could I not? Especially as Dr Friedman began, '*Dear Friend*'. To the Executive Director, I am more even than a fellow Earthling. He likes me.

'*Dear Friend,*

As someone lured by the immense complexity of the universe, you may not realize that humankind is about to enter a new generation of space travel.'

My neck hairs rose. How on earth – as it were – did Dr Friedman know that I was lured by the immense complexity of the universe? Not everyone is. I have heard of people who, when shown how a pea moves round an orange, or possibly vice-versa, every – was it 24 hours? – found their attention wandering. What mysterious force had persuaded my new friend Dr Friedman that I counted myself something of a buff in such matters?

Rapt, I read on, and exhilarating stuff it was. Although Dr Friedman charmingly confessed, '*No, I can't reserve for you a spot on a planetary mission . . . yet*', his revelation that the society was already designing a balloon to be used on Mars held out such hope of imminent interplanetary awaydays as to make the pitch, when it inevitably came, nugatory: an annual subscription of less than £20, to ensure by return a smart membership card which will unquestionably allow one to shove to the front of the queue when the midnight choo-choo leaves for Aldebaran.

Little wonder that President Sagan exhorted me to spread the word! Why, he even included my acceptance letter, neatly typeset, and pitched at exactly the level of discreet gratitude I myself would have chosen: *'Thank you, Carl Sagan,'* my letter replied, *'for inviting me to join you for this new age of space exploration. I want to be part of the ultimate adventure – the exploration of our solar system and beyond, and the search for extraterrestrial intelligence. My $30 dollar payment is enclosed.'*

I hesitated over signing it, mind: it was the *'and beyond'* which gave me pause. I am as keen as the next man to shell out thirty bucks for the chance to stroll Pluto, but a commitment to ballooning through Deep Space with only a Pasadena credit reference as my passport is a risk I do not feel ready to take. Intelligent extraterrestrial life there may well be, but what guarantee is there that they believe in Carl Sagan?

Wiser, perhaps, to invest in a hired spruce? Since one is so rarely offered the choice between inter-galactic tourism and tree-rental, a letter received on Tuesday from Bill & Ben's Greenhouse, 385 Euston Road, proved more than usually imponderable. Despite eschewing their endearing obbalob-dobbalob mode of yesteryear, Bill and Ben still succeeded in leaving the brain in ruins.

'We attach two photographs of the Christmas tree special we are offering this Yule tide. Unfortunately, the photographs are of a nasty artificial tree which is not to be compared with the Abies Normanniana (bushy, Norwegian, non-needle drop) tree we shall provide. However, you do get an idea of the effect the decorations will create. These are top quality, all the way from the U.S. of A, including hand-painted baubles with wooden novelties.'

All the way from Pasadena, was my first suspicious thought, designed to look a treat in the corner of the balloon as Professor Carl Sagan and I traversed Mars, wassailing. But no: this tree was not for keeping, it was for hire. Bill and Ben, their *billet-doux* continued, would '*supply a fully-decked 6-foot tree to one of three themes, namely Love Geese (blue and silver), Naughty Teddy (green and gold), and See-Thru Glass (silver and white). We hope to deliver all trees by the end of the first week of December, inclusive of smart stand and drinking water. Trees and decorations will be collected at the beginning of January. You pay us £125.*'

Or don't. Even with drinking-water thrown in, £125 strikes me as a bit steep for hiring a 6-foot Norwegian tree. I would expect to hire a 6-foot Norwegian for that, just the thing for seeing Yuletide drunks off the premises, keeping the front path snowless, and mopping up any turkey risotto still hanging about on Twelfth Night. He wouldn't have Love Geese or Naughty Teddies hanging on him, of course, but there's a bright side to everything.

DECEMBER

I have nothing against the skip *qua* skip. Until it came along, not only were urban kerbs depressingly inanimate, domestic archaeology was open only to those prepared to sign on at one of the more progressive polytechnics. Nowadays, the rich history of cistern and mattress is graphically available to all. These little oblong museums have become both part of our national heritage and faithful servants of it.

Just the other day, for example, I learned more than I even knew I should need to know about double-glazing. Attracted by the twinkling splinters around one of our neighbourhood favourites, I peered inside and caught my breath at as creative an arabesque of aluminium angles as I had ever seen. Had the 1988 Turner Prize not already been settled, I should have had the skip hauled round to the Tate before you could say Anthony Caro and emptied it on to the step, where the curators of our culture would have been only too happy to refill it with fivers.

I had hardly begun to enjoy it, however, before a labourer came out of the house behind it and quoted me his asking price for the scrap. I shall have to get a better tailor. Anyway, having set him right, I asked him why anyone should rip out of a houseful of perfectly good windows, and received in return perhaps the most fascinating lecture on the double glazing of the Macmillan Era I have ever had the privilege of hearing.

It used to stick a lot, apparently.

It is not the skips themselves to which I object, but their civil rights. I live in a part of London where, should you park briefly on a yellow line, the solution to the problem you represent to traffic flow is represented either by a wheel-clamp (which renders your obstruction permanent) or a mobile police crane (which closes off the road just long enough to winch up your vehicle and establish a nine-mile traffic jam from Finchley to Wandsworth). If you put a skip on the yellow line, however, no one touches it, despite the fact that it is half as wide again as your car and will be there for anything up to six months. Enquiring at West Hampstead police station, I discovered that this dispensation is automatic, upon application to the council for a skip licence. The police have no interest in the skip, unless it fails to display a light at night.

Since most of the forbidden parking spots I need have legitimized skips on them, my course would thus seem to be clear. I shall designate my car a skip. I shall then apply for a licence to deposit a skip on a yellow line. Provided I leave the boot open so that honest citizens may sidle up during the night and fill it with old lavatories, I don't see how Plod can touch me.

O n Monday evening, at what I fear will be the first of umpteen Yuletide opportunities for strangers to honk at one another over vols-au-vents while doing their best not to step on those who have slid senseless to the Wilton, I suddenly found myself face to face with Lord Eccles, whom I had last met in the company, during his heyday, of a hapless mutual friend currently poised to explain himself to an Old Bailey jury. There was a reflective pause.

'I have the biggest collection of Staffordshire plaques in the country,' said Lord Eccles, finally.

Tact is the mortar of society.

I have a bee, and I do not know what to do with it. Though not perhaps a household word where apiarists forgather, I have none the less always had rather a soft spot for bees, and I should like to do right by this one, which needs me. It doesn't

80

know it needs me, but *I* know it needs me, and I have no intention of making it suffer for an atheism not of its choosing. Just as God's eye is, as I understand it, on the sparrow, mine is on the bee.

And the bee's is on the carpet. It has been there for two days, ambling around, buzzing spasmodically, and occasionally taking off for a lumbering circuit of the room. When it lands, it rolls about a bit. It is clearly in poor nick. Now, does this mean it is also in agony? And, if so, would the kindest course be to step on it? The option is to evict it into a freezing world, where it would die in considerably less comfort, probably eaten by robins, a way few of us would choose to go.

The bee is exceedingly unlucky in falling into a rather special bracket. Were it a less benevolent insect – a wasp, a flea, an earwig – my course would be simpler: though morally no more defensible, swatting it would at least carry the teleological excuse of doing it to it before it did it to me. Were it a bit bigger – a gerbil, a toad, a guppie – I could pass the buck vetwards, but I cannot quite bring myself to sit in a waiting-room with a matchbox on my knee and invite the derision of skinheads with duff wolfhounds.

My son thinks the only honourable course is to pick it up so that it can sting me and die fulfilled. Personally, I can't see how ending up with two things crawling around on the carpet would solve much.

Say what you like about the Duke of Edinburgh, when it comes to addressing life's prime cruces there is no chap I would rather have at my elbow. The First Man – if Denis Thatcher will forgive me – has a knack of winkling out the nub of things which leaves the lesser thinker breathless.

Take last Tuesday, when, in one of his jollier fulminations, he drew a remarkable distinction anent the manufacture of meat. The philippic pith was couched, admittedly, in an analogy about wives and prostitutes so convoluted as to leave even the smartest of structuralists crawling on all fours towards the nearest vodka, but his point, when it came, was needle-sharp. The world, according to the great consort, was split up into hunters and butchers: hunters did it for fun, butchers did it for money.

It meant – this is often the way with major truths – little to me at the time. But a week on, it means everything. Last Saturday, I went, for the first time in my life, shooting. More accurately – a word for which the day itself turned out to have scant use – I went walking behind a number of gentlemen who had gone shooting.

They were a convivial and charming group, drawn neither from the ornithocidal gentry who grow misty for the days when George V would shoot his own weight in woodcock before his first cheroot had dwindled, nor from the yuppie-come-latelies who have learned to fire one-handed in order to remain in unbroken portaphone contact with the Hong Kong bourse, but from the genial ranks of decent sporting businessfolk able respectably to raise £300 for a day's banging away.

Indeed, the whole affair was manifestly businesslike, keynoted by a locale which could hardly have been a further cry from the romantic wildness of the sporting aquatint, sited as it was in the permanent lee of Fawley oil refinery. The day saw eight different drives, but every drive saw Fawley's towering concrete. Since our little platoon was ported from drive to drive in the back of a Land Rover, and since at each halt the vehicle debouched a dozen men in khaki jackets who immediately began firing in the general direction of the oil industry, our party resembled nothing so much as a small band of guerrillas dropped into suburban Hampshire by an unnamed foreign power and committed to striking at the heart of Britain's energy.

What they were firing in the specific direction of, however, was pheasant. Bred to die, the hand-fed targets ambled from cover, hopped up briefly in the air, and flapped slowly into a barrage of pellets which accounted, astonishingly, for very few of them. Those struck fell around me to lie like feathered reticules, whereupon highly trained dogs began running away from them. I took Prince Philip's point immediately. It was enormous fun, if you liked that sort of thing . . .

At the end of the shoot, I was, though a non-combatant, generously given a brace of pheasant, cock and hen strung together at the neck in a rather touching eternal embrace. I put them in the boot. When I arrived home, I hung them on a nail in the garage, and invited my wife to take a look.

'They appear to be full,' she said.

'Yes, they come down like that,' I said expertly. 'You have to pluck the outside stuff off and pull the inside stuff out.'

She went back into the house. I looked at the pheasants for a bit.

My local butcher, Mr Kingsland, shook his head. 'This time of year?' he said. 'Couldn't touch it. There's just me and the boy.'

'Couldn't touch it,' said the boy, 'this time of year.'

'Any other time,' said Mr Kingsland.

'There's all these turkeys,' said the boy.

I came out of the shop into West End Lane. It was Monday, and the weather was warm, but the pheasant were all right, so far. A few feathers fell out when I put them back in the boot.

I tried four other butchers on the way to my office and three on the way home. It turned out to be this time of year. Only one, the Al Madina in Crawford Street, went mad: simply walking into a halal butcher's with a couple of moulting cadavers can render the entire premises unholy, apparently. You learn something every day.

When I opened the boot on Tuesday afternoon outside Somers & Kirby, Connaught Street, to which a kindly but otherwise unhelpful soul in Selfridge's had directed me, something was definitely up. You did not need to be a bloodhound. I carried them in, at arm's length.

'Could you come back Friday?' said either Somers or Kirby. 'Can't promise, mind.'

I looked at the pheasants. More feathers fell off.

It is Wednesday, as I write. The pheasants are back on the nail. Ian McCaskill has just said the weather is unseasonally warm, but I already knew.

I have made more phone calls today, and there's something else I know. Which is that the gulf between hunters and butchers would appear to be wider even than the Duke's steely perception can encompass. Butchers don't even do it for money, if someone else has done it for fun.

hey are all gone into the world of light, and I alone sit lingering here . . . well, you would expect reverberant quotations to pop up in lieu of original expression, would you not, in a middle-aged graduate caught ambling the moonlit quad of his old college, thirty years on, all mortals down for the Christmas vacation and nothing dancing on the grass but ghosts?

Especially as quotations are all I seem to have left of what I learned here. Time was, chapter and verse were merely minor constituents of study, deployed to render cockeyed theory plausible. It was the theory that counted. Once – when the brain was lean and fit and quick on its pins – if you'd suggested to me that Crabbe was not the last Augustan but the first Romantic, or that Thackeray owed nothing to Peacock, I should have come out fighting. Not any longer. When I finally pushed my handcart lifewards over Magdalen Bridge in 1961, it was piled high with smart intellectual luggage, but as the adult road grew rougher, almost everything fell off. All I have now is an old carrier-bag with a few resonant couplets in, and even that's getting lighter by the minute. In fact, I shouldn't have been in Wadham at all, last Saturday evening. I had come up for the St Thomas's Day Dinner in New College, but I had arrived early and needed to kill time.

I ought to have realized that that is all too precisely what you do when you step back through a doorway you stepped out of an aeon earlier. Even so, I think I should have been able to cope with the inadvertently summoned spirits had I not, on wandering into Wadham's Chapel Quad, suddenly been confronted by Sir Maurice Bowra, dead these seventeen years yet lit, now, by a shaft of moonlight, recalling nothing so much as the resurrection, in his Viennese doorway, of Harry Lime. I blinked, but he was still there, outside my head, not in it.

It was, as Coleridge murmured from the carrier-bag, a sight to dream of, not to tell. Sir Maurice had come back as a chair. While I had heard that a bronze statue had been commissioned to commemorate the great Warden, I had not realized that the sculptor had chucked in the smock halfway through, leaving the job to be finished off by Habitat. There is the head and torso, accurate enough, bull-solid as in life, but it stops at the waist: below, cheap chairlegs. It is not only appalling in itself, it is an invitation to disrespect. You can sit in Bowra's lap. You can stand on him to look over the wall. If you had a folding table, you could, according to my carrier-bag, take your little porringer and eat your supper there.

What on earth was the selection committee up to? Is it some ghastly pun about the academic chair Bowra never had, do there lurk within this travesty mischievous personal allusions which the uninitiated can only guess at, or is it simply a matter of crude revenge being taken on one who, admittedly, accumulated more enemies than it is circumspect to leave behind?

How is a critic to deconstruct this artefact? More to the point, when will someone do it literally?

Muttering back into the main quad, I noticed a soft glow that had not been there ten minutes before. *'But soft!'* said the carrier-bag, *'What light through yonder window breaks?'*

Figures seemed to have taken up residence in one of the ground-floor lecture rooms. I walked across and peered in. Some twenty men and women lay on tables, in various states of undress, having their arms and legs pulled about by some twenty more. Grunting rattled the mullions. An experimental drama group, perhaps, giving up their vacation to interpret some modish Latvian absurdist? College oarspersons limbering up for the imminent season? Members of The Civil Defence Monday Club demonstrating their suspicion of *glasnost* by preparing for the aftermath of a nuclear blitz?

I was still speculating when a small but effectively designed blonde girl emerged from the neighbouring doorway. I inquired. She replied: *'Quoi?'* Slipping effortlessly into incomprehensible French in the hope that, as I gabbled, the carrier-bag might dredge up something suitably seductive from the 1954 O level set texts, thereby enabling me to spend a more diverting Sunday than I had anticipated – defrost a punt, scrounge a ukelele, introduce her to Scotch eggs, all that – I succeeded only in discovering that she was an osteopath.

There were dozens of them, convened thither from all over France. It was how the college made ends meet.

During the drinking that followed the astonishing New College dinner – whatever the carrier-bag's views on foie gras to the sound of trumpets, I am here to tell you that guinea-fowl to the sound of a galleried choir has it by the short head – I mentioned my unease at Wadham's boarders to the don beside me, recalling that in my day (a phrase I could not have used more than thirty or forty times that night), vacationing groups were invariably foreign academics with whom the hosting Fellows could chew the academic fat to useful professional effect. They weren't bloody chiropractors.

'Wadham's fortunate,' he replied. 'We've got Japanese toy manufacturers in ours. Yesterday they were throwing little lorries out of the window to see if they'd break.'

And see, his eyes are flat with change, murmured the carrier-bag.

Three days on, and despite the elegantly couched promises in which it was wrapped, my dancing cane still refuses to follow me around room in big mystery. It does not dance where I go. It does not astound all who look on it.

All who look on it say, 'Why are you pulling that stick round on a string?'

I have a mind to take it back to Taiwan and bung it at the proprietor of Mr Chu's Quality Magic. Though not perhaps a household word where international jurists forgather, I am nevertheless pretty certain that you cannot accept folding money for items which, contrary to undertakings on lid, do not dance where you go. Especially when you have spent most of Christmas morning sitting cross-legged in a nest of wrapping paper attempting to assemble something only marginally less fragmented than the Portland Vase, so that, when you try to get up again, it takes some considerable time to discover that your dancing cane will not follow you around room in big mystery, because you cannot get round room yourself, except on all fours, thanks to big mystery of no joints working.

I cannot get the egg out of the egg bag either. It should be simple, according to Mr Chu's lucid assurances: *Take bag, take*

*egg, put egg in bag, turn bag inside out, lo, egg has vanished!
Ask friends: Where is egg?*

I do not know what Mr Chu's friends answer at this point; it
may be that either gullibility or social discretion is different Out
East. Mr Chu's friends could well, when asked, be either
astounded by big mystery or generously affecting same. I know
only that my friends immediately answer: *Egg in bag, lo, can see
egg-shaped lump at bottom of bag!*

This tends to pre-empt Part Two of Mr Chu's instructions:
Now you produce egg with flourish! Worse. In my case, *now you
not find egg in bag. Now you only person present unable to
answer: Where is egg? Egg there somewhere, can see egg
dangling, can feel egg, but cannot get egg out with flourish or
anything else. All who look on it astounded you not able to get
egg out. Put egg-bag in pocket. Egg now follow you around room
in big mystery.*

By Boxing Day, who could not begin to suspect ulterior
motives in those of my family who had persuaded Santa to lash
his reindeer halfway round the world in search of Mr Chu's Giant
Magical Chest? Whenever interest in old movies flagged,
whenever anyone woke – or sobered – up, their first reaction was
to ask me to get my present out and do the Amazing Milk Trick
again. The Amazing Milk Trick consists of pouring a pint of milk
into one of Mr Chu's tumblers, turning the tumbler upside down,
and running off to get a floor-cloth. I have thought about this for
some time and reached the conclusion that this is not a failed
trick at all; this is a successful trick designed by Mr Chu to evoke
the response – engagingly described in his booklet as *All present
laugh loud!* – not forthcoming from the trick to which it refers,
should this fail.

The trick is called Funny Teeth. The rubric is simple: *Leave
room. Insert Funny Teeth. Go back in room and smile. All
present laugh loud!*

Perhaps, in Taiwan, they do. In Cricklewood, all present just
look at you, especially if you go back in room and choke.

It may be that the Chinese Nationalist mouth is differently
configured from the European, which might also go some way
towards explaining my inability to confuse all hearers that a beast

is present.

According to Mr Chu, his Wonderful Double Swiss Warbler can imitate any beast, despite the fact that it looks like a corn plaster. *Directions for use: Soak in water until thoroughly blown up, then place on tongue with reed nearest teeth* (own, presumably, not Funny) *and finished side of leather upwards, and hiss gently, giving imitation of Beast. Any person following these instructions we will guarantee they can surprise all present that a Beast is here. Take care not to swallow. Keep away from children.*

The final injunction is the wisest. If there is anything that a magician wishing to pass himself off as a Beast should keep away from, it's children. If he does not, all present cry: 'Why is that man spitting all over everywhere, why is his face going purple?'

God knows best what beast Mr Chu's Wonderful Double Swiss Warbler is supposed to sound like. It is, I suppose, just possible that the beast is actually a double swiss warbler, a creature which gives off a sort of strangled gurgle, and that I am doing it absolutely correctly. All I know is that none present cocked an ear and exclaimed 'I say, can anyone see a double swiss warbler? I swear I heard one just now.'

There is only one trick left in the box this Wednesday afternoon. It is in a round blue tin, the size of a shoe polish container. On the lid there is this legend: *Big Gas Fright.* On the bottom of the tin, the instructions read: *Remove lid, there is a candle. Hide candle in safe place and light. Soon comes a smell of leaking gas. All present run about.*

Call me poltroon if you will, Mr Chu, but I should cocoa.

JANUARY

I have taken another job. Quite literally, I moonlight. The job is in the 18th century. I do not have the uniform yet, because it is not easy to lay contemporary hands on a reinforced tricorn hat, or a bespoke cloak, or a big brass handbell, or a regulation knobkerry; but I wear them in spirit. My lantern may live on Duracell, but in its heart it dreams of naphtha.

I am a Neighbourhood Watchman. It is unquestionably the most glorious new career generated by the self-sufficiency culture. It reaches back beyond even Victorian values to a time when the swift despatch of footpad and highwayman was left to Englishmen civic-minded enough to go nowhere without swordstick and horse-pistol.

I am not, of course, allowed any such prosthesis to my short legal arm, but in the event of spotting anything dodgy upon my nocturnal rounds, I am, by the power vested in me, fully entitled to run home, lock myself in, and dial 999.

Unfortunately, that dodginess proved, over the holiday period, to be immeasurably more difficult to spot than I had anticipated. Hardly had our Neighbourhood Watch scheme been set up – monitory stickers in windows, nickable items covertly marked with cabbalistic runes, keys duplicated and keyholders nominated, tea and buns shared with cheery young policemen, surveillance rosters drawn up, and all that – than the entire Neighbourhood left the country.

Just before Christmas, they dressed their trees, wreathed their doors, gave every ostentatious sign to putative villainy that they would be in permanent residence, and then hopped it to sun and snow, leaving me with a cupboardful of keys to a dozen different alarm systems and a drawerful of hastily scribbled instructions as to the idiosyncrasies of each, plus whose cat was being fed on what by whom, which plumber could be trusted in the event of burst pipes, which elderly ladies in floral hats would legitimately be fumbling with unfamiliar Yales in order to water aspidistras (as compared with those who were bent on prising the wall safe from its moorings), and so on.

All quite straightforward, really, except for two things. The first was that the holidaymakers had neglected to tell me – can it be that I myself am not wholly trusted? – that half their precautionary kit was not as stated and that the other half was on the blink. I have thus, in my new job, passed the hardest-working fortnight of my entire life.

It was not merely the innumerable false alarms set clanging by sensitivity to rust, damp, loneliness, or whatever other caprice takes wiring's fancy in the small hours, forcing me to leap from my mattress, grasp fistfuls of keys, and canter the streets like Wee Willie Winkie in order to identify first the culprit and then its key; it was not merely the second stage of this enterprise which was to ensure before entering that there was no external sign that someone had entered before me and thus that the wild goose I was chasing was not waiting behind the door with a sockful of sand – all of which takes a considerable amount of time, nervous energy and, if job commitment has prevented you from pulling socks on, body heat; it was not merely padding about unfamiliar premises, knocking breakables over in the search for light switches, to enable me to read instructions which would turn out to be for the house four doors away; it was not even not being able to remember, in one case, whether the cat that seemed to have triggered an alarm by going in through its catflap should have been there at all or whether it should have been with the people up the road; or whether, indeed, it had standing instructions to water the aspidistra.

It was far more than all this. It was, for example, not having

92

been informed that one particular alarm system was linked to Golders Green nick, so that when two policemen turned up in an unmarked red Astra at 3 am, it took some considerable time to establish not only that I was who I was but that they were who they were (even so, the current much publicized rash of bogus fuzz meant that I insisted on checking the house with them, so that we went from room to room watching one another like hawks).

It was, for example, not having been forewarned that at least two of my neighbours had timing devices which turned lights on and off at pre-set moments, so that not only did I, during my maiden nocturnal round, initiate a highly embarrassing line of police inquiry, but that ever thereafter I had no idea whether the lights were going on and off of their own accord or whether intruders were doing it manually.

Worst of all, I was coming – after the first fraught week – to the unsettling conclusion that there was a dangerously insecure grey area which lay between the shrill clanging of real alarms and false alarms; for it had struck me that the smartest course a villain could take would be to trigger an alarm and then sprint to a vantage point from which he could observe Neighbourhood Watchmen and policemen shouting at one another until such time as they had convinced themselves of a fault in the system, and that if it went off again they would ignore it and try to get such remnants of sleep as the cowboy security trade had left them.

I t being the grisly season when the *soi-disant* stars of stage, screen and analyst's couch forgather to weep on one another's dinner jackets and accept gilt doorstops for prancing about, how satisfying it was to turn down simultaneous invitations for both the Laurence Olivier Awards and the Evening Standard Film Awards and to address oneself instead to the discreet ceremony for The Pet of the Year.

Here there was no oleaginous self-acclamatory mewing, no specious gratitude for the unsung gerbils behind the scenes without whom this or that gong would not have been possible, no hoary old jokes ineptly yapped off a prompt card by some arthritic American collie basketed over from Hollywood specially for the occasion to defy the soapy suggestion that he needed no introduction.

The Pet of the Year sat silently, with no more than half his tongue hanging decorously out, as a small beribboned medal was placed around his neck. The medal said JACOB. Jacob is a German Shepherd (I have never understood why they aren't called German sheepdogs. What do the Germans call shepherds?) who, I was delighted to learn, received his award for 'loyalty and devotion to his mistress'.

How rare that is, these days! Once upon a time, even a king would cry 'Let not poor Nellie starve!' and leave her an acre or two of downtown real estate to tide her over any shortfall in orange futures, and to hell with public opinion.

But today not even a third-rate politician, no matter which side of the Atlantic you may scour, is prepared to stand by his bimbo when the *paparazzi* start firing. It takes a dog to show us the way, and a Jerry one, at that.

My own involvement with the animal kingdom has prospered ill this week. At Christmas my daughter made me the father of a pelican. She coughed up the wherewithal which ensured that not only would a Dalmatian exemplar henceforth be housed and foraged in my name at the London Zoo, but also that a smart plaque to this effect would stand by its pond so that the world would know who its old man was.

What with one thing and another, though, it was Monday before I could get around to dropping in on him, to bung him a herring and break the news that he was adopted.

But when finally I managed to part the sleet in front of the pelican enclosure and peer through, there was no sign of the plaque. There was no shortage of pelicans, many of them quite possibly Dalmatian, and not a few plaques testifying to such various parentages as the Midland Bank and a primary school in, as I recall, Hornchurch. But none with my name on.

So I put the herring back in my pocket and trudged over to the zoo office, where a sympathetic young woman said there had indeed been a plaque up, but that it had disappeared. It happened all the time. There was a lot of it about.

What kind of bastard, I inquired, nicks a pelican's birth certificate? It turned out that zoo plaques make ideal photo-frames, providing you are prepared to take the trouble to jemmy them off the railings and shove them under your anorak, rather than shell out £1.95 in W.H. Smith.

So I went home and put the herring in the fridge. A new plaque, I was given to understand, will go up next month; though for how long, no one, in these troubled times, was prepared to say.

I reached a watershed on Tuesday. Speaking as one who has stood athwart The Great Divide and realized that the rain falling on his left shoe would eventually drain into the Pacific while the rain falling on his right would drain into the Atlantic, I do not use the cliché lightly. Tuesday was a big day. For the first time in my life, I took a bath with the door unlocked. More remarkable yet, I locked it, got into the bath, thought for a bit, got out again, unlocked it, and got back in.

This is of so little interest that I feel you ought to know it could save your life; also your decor. What had occurred to me in between getting in and getting out was that I had, at that very moment, reached the age at which the possibility of a heart attack was no longer an actuarial niggle to boost premiums. If it happened in the bath, I wanted someone to be able to act upon my first shriek, blow down my throat, jump on my sternum, all that stuff. If the door was locked, they would not be able to do it. It is a sturdy door, and opens outwards.

The fire brigade would have to be called. They would take time. The world's last view of me would be sitting naked in the conjoined palms of two firemen, stiff as a board and dripping. What their axes would do to the tiling did not bear thinking about.

I should not wish to end without offering my congratulations to President Ceausescu on becoming Hero of Romania, his country's highest honour, which he has just awarded himself. No braver man ever deserved the title: my sources in Bucharest tell me that his attempt to kiss himself on both cheeks was prevented only on the intervention of his osteopath.

The billboards opposite my office are a bleak bellwether of the times. Across their changing face, cultural signals pass which weigh the heart and drag it bootwards. I am coming to believe that Old Nick has bought the site concession in order to offset the cheery gobbets gummed up outside the church next door with spiritually downlifting messages of his own. Some days, I daren't look out of the window.

On Monday, I watched two men strip the sad remains of a launch campaign for *Riva*, a women's magazine which lasted six weeks at the cost of as many millions, and replace them. Between the neighbour hoardings – an advertisement for Dunhill cigarettes whose sales pitch was based on the information that 30,000 people in the UK died each year from lung cancer, and a picture of Sir Cyril Smith whose inability to touch his toes was supposed to encourage us to take advantage of the greater flexibility of Access to put ourselves in Carey Street – 300 square feet of new blandishment slowly dried into place.

On the new poster's left, a giant American footballer. On its right, a giant parrot. Beneath, the word 'Bournemouth' and the number 0933 401501. I stared at this horrible thing for a bit, balancing curiosity against self-esteem. This is a cheap trick designed to con me into telephoning, I thought; and telephoned.

The man at the other end had not heard the one about the footballer and the parrot. He was merely answering, he said, on behalf of 0202 291715. Do not ask me why 0202 291715 could not have put its own number on the hoarding. Pressed, I might offer guesses about BT wanting to make even more money by getting twerps to make two phone calls where one would do.

I twerped.

I had explained as far as the parrot when the woman said: 'You want Judith Pratt.'

How did she know? Even I didn't know I wanted Judith Pratt.

'Hello,' said Judith Pratt.

After I had described what had been defined as the nature of my call, Judith Pratt said: 'There is a whole strategy of thinking behind the imagery.'

I told her that I was sure there was, but what was it about?

'It is about repositioning Bournemouth in the holiday market,' said Judith.

There are moments when you can actually feel the iron enter your soul.

Bournemouth, Judith expatiated, had too long been perceived as a spot where the elderly trundled one another around in bathchairs. It was time to change all that. Many people, for example, didn't know that Bournemouth had its own American football team. Had I heard of The Bournemouth Bobcats? I trawled the memory, in vain.

'What about the parrot?' I said. 'It wasn't a parrot,' cried Judith, with all the ornithological confidence of someone who has been in on the whole strategy of thinking from its very inception, it was a lovebird. Many people did not know that Bournemouth had its own exotic aviary.

'And have you,' she continued, even as I staggered, 'heard of the Lower Pleasure Gardens?'

Sadly, the first of those three capital letters turned out, on inquiry, to be mine. It is not the pleasure which is lower, but the gardens. Still, it may not be too late to look again at the whole strategy of thinking: if line-backers and lovebirds unaccountably fail to reposition Bournemouth in the holiday market, the introduction of a few carefully researched lower pleasures might be just the ticket.

Let us, mind, not be too snooty about image refurbishment. Some quite decent people are prepared to go out on this risky limb. For Christmas, my wife bought me a hat. That is to say, we had a long and highly seasonal lunch at Wilton's, and then walked as best we could around the St James's corner to Lock & Co, Hatters, where for 20 minutes the memory of the great Tommy Cooper was celebrated in – though the word may not be entirely appropriate – style. Even the patience of Mr Lock's shimmering helpers, however, is not infinitely testable, and the moment of reckoning had to come, in this case £72 for a broad-brimmed, donkey-hued number which – if you wish to picture this – would have suited Humphrey Bogart to a T.

It suited me to about C. The fact that I had never had a hat before made it impossible to judge whether I was wise to have one now, because as soon as I put it on I ceased to be the person I had formerly been, and had no way of knowing whether it was the right hat for the person it had made me become. We are talking Wittgensteinian millinery here.

The hat has led to certain problems out on the street, undiminished after three fraught weeks. Not only do I consistently glance sidelong into windows, at considerable threat to safe forward passage, but I also stare at the other men in hats, to find out if I am doing it right. Usually they ignore me – although from the occasional half-smile I guess there is unquestionably a small Fellowship of the Hat – but on occasion they stare back very hard at mine. I have thought about this, and conclude that those who stare back hard are themselves wearing new hats.

As insights go, it may not be much; but of such tiny chips is life's rich mosaic composed.

The joy of surrealism is that, though its reverberations are complex, its constituents are simple. For example, early last Saturday morning, as I waited at traffic lights in Gloucester Place, a police constable crossed, slowly, in front of my car. He was carrying a violin case.

Speculation, of course, burst like shrapnel. Is there a Serious Crimes Quintet that convenes each weekend to saw away at Boccherini and Franck? Has Clause 28 swung into operation overnight, requiring all gay buskers to hand over their offensive weapons? Or am I merely witnessing the caring method by which the Met bears tommy-guns across its patch, so as not to alarm the innocent? Indeed, might it even be that catgut itself has now been pressed into the fight against violence, and that Plod was off to Millwall, where – in the event of a riot – a few bars of *These Foolish Things* would soothe the savage supporter?

Then again, was he, perhaps, not a real policeman at all, but some recherché fetishist scuttling to an arcane tryst at the nearby

Churchill Hotel, where the violin would soon be cover-driving meringues pitched at its owner by a big-busted leg-spinner in a lurex tuxedo? None of this mattered. Here, quite simply, was a conjunction of copper and violin. Magritte himself could not have asked for more.

There is an even more puzzling uniform standing guard outside Wellington Barracks. As you would expect, it clothes a busbied sentry, and as you would further expect, he is stern of mien, unflinching of gaze, and does not budge or mutter when dogs abuse his impeccable toe-cap.

It may strike you as odd that he is alone, when Welly B offers not only a somewhat long façade for one man to keep an eye on, but also unrivalled photo-opportunities for the tourist hordes who trudge thither to capture on emulsion the ceremonial treats which have seduced them, at vast expense, from Oslo and Des Moines. It will strike you as even odder when I tell you that he is made of plywood.

Crossing St James's Park at the weekend, I noticed that a loose Nipponese knot had formed around this solitary custodian of our heritage. Half-a-dozen lens-hung visitors were staring at him, and I could just catch, from the other side of Birdcage Walk, an exchange of baffled ideograms. After a bit, one of the Japs prodded the guardsman with his forefinger. The guardsman rocked. The visitors hooted. They then began taking it in turns to form up and photograph one another with their arms around him.

What on earth is happening? Have we fallen so low that we can no longer muster even one thin red individual to stand between us and foreign humiliation? Maybe we have no army at all, merely serried ranks of Queen's Own Chipboard Light Infantry and 17th/21st Rubber Foot, stacked in tea-chests to be opened in the event of invasion to give the enemy a bit of a fright. Or giggle.

I think someone should tell me. I have forked out a bob or two on defence down the years, I don't mind saying.

I have, however, forked out nothing on defence against the latest foreign intruder, Hurricane K. Having, along with everyone else, railed against the Met Office's failure to warn us of The Last Lot,

I find myself on Tuesday morning waking to radio prophecies of such Sybilline intensity and detail about The Next Lot as to leave the nerves in tatters. It is the metmen's revenge: still smarting from their poor reviews, the McCaskills and Fishes have cried: *'They want warnings? OK, we'll give 'em warnings!'* knowing that the majority of the queendom is in no position to do anything with the warnings it has been given.

Had I a boat, I suppose I could shove it in the lee of something; had I a nervous herd, I should probably pop some patent sedative in its feed to forestall curdling or miscarriage; but being, like most of us, a mid-urban man, what possible use can I make of the information issuing from the radio even as I type, except run hysterically around like Stan Laurel?

In The Last Lot, my roof desquamated. What do I do now? Sellotape all the tiles down? Three sturdy trees blew over; shall I enjoin the rest to hold hands, lean into the wind, and sing something to keep their spirits, and their limbs, up? I lost a fence; shall I spend the day running from one end of its replacement to the other like a Chinese juggler keeping two dozen plates spinning atop their bamboo poles, or stay indoors, so as to earn the wherewithal to foot the imminent timber bills? Shall I simply up sticks and caravan the family to some more clement billet?

There is nothing to be done. The magnificent final paragraph of Sam Johnson's *Rasselas* springs ringingly to mind. *Of these wishes that they had formed they well knew that none could be obtained. They deliberated awhile what was to be done and resolved when the inundation should cease, to return to Abyssinia.*

I am delighted to announce that the Most Erotic Statue in London Competition has been won by Sir Arthur Sullivan's. It stands in the Victoria Embankment Gardens, between the Savoy and the Thames. Susceptible men visit at their peril.

It is that time of year when authors walk abroad in false beards. Those uncircumspect enough to own real beards walk abroad hardly at all, and then only under cover of darkness, hugging the walls and jinking past street lamps with startlingly devious nippiness.

For it is National Agoraphobia Week in the scribbling trade. That is because last week was National Print-Out Week, when those who scratch a fraught living at the unyielding wordface receive their annual performance-report: *The Public Lending Right Statement of Earnings*. As a statement of earnings, it is, of course, nugatory: even that handful of rat-faced, time-serving, lickspittle running dogs of W.H. Smith who have sold their birthright for a mess of bestsellers cannot receive more than the threshold £6,000 – which this year goes to 67 of them, to whom the remaining 15,967 of us offer this heartfelt good wish, that they do not choke horribly to death on the celebratory caviare they honestly, really, no truly, do so richly deserve.

So then, since the top money is but an annual starvation wage, why do the 15,967 who don't get it spend these bleak days huddled at home in front of their roaring *Angst*, with their telephones off the hook, each refusing to venture out for fear of bumping into one of the other 15,966? The clue lies in the colour chosen by the PLR Office for the print-out. It is green.

What authors envy most is not sales, but readership. True, they may cast a sidelong jaundiced eye at the monogrammed Ferraris of those in whose household names whole Finnish hillsides have been felled, but the axiomatic definition of the best-seller for those who do not write them is that they are all junk. Indeed, the self-esteem of the quality writer depends on his belief that those readers who care about good stuff cannot afford to buy it. From which, unfortunately, follows the downside of the PLR for which quality writers fought so long: the *Statement of Earnings* is actually a measurement of the discriminating poor who batten upon their local libraries for literary nourishment. The annual PLR print-out thus informs the recipient whether he was deemed worth reading by those he deemed worth writing for.

Which is why 15,967 citizens are currently attempting to avoid one another. If they fail to avoid one another, they will have to talk about the encirclement of Kabul or the price of sprouts. They will not even be able to look one another in the eye, for fear of seeing something to their disadvantage.

I went for a walk on Hampstead Heath last Sunday morning

and it was as vacant as the moon. True, from time to time bearded things would break cover, but they had invariably gained the next little copse before I could, from their atypical crouching scuttle, identify them.

Nor is it simply a fear of external comparison which harrows us: the internal scale is no less fretful. In fact, it may actually be of less concern to us that Melvyn's or Julian's books were snatched more frequently off the municipal shelves than ours, compared with whether the snatching of ours was more or less frequent than it was a year ago. Are we on the up, or on the down? Of course, if we have any sense, we have forgotten where we filed last year's PLR sheet, and if we are really smart, we have further forgotten its bottom line, but a survey recently carried out, albeit inside my own head, showed that of 16,034 authors interviewed, only 67 neither knew nor cared what they had registered in 1988.

Still, literary quality rarely receives its deserts. Otherwise, the Whitbread Prize must surely have gone to Mr Rottenberg.

Though but an architect, Mr Rottenberg (of Rottenberg Associates) is one of the great prose stylists of our time. Passing his signboard at 24 Avenue Road, St John's Wood, I was forced to clutch at the half-finished wall of his Pavilions site, so ringingly unfettered was the sentence with which he was hawking it: *An exceptional development of the most select and unique apartments, each one offering superb amenities for the ultimate in living.*

Leave to wittering philosophers abstract speculation anent man's endless search! Mr Rottenberg knows that the ultimate in living is a pile of ochre brickwork in NW8, and is not afraid to come right out and say so, in prose which makes the molars rattle.

These days, I rarely give long shrift to the felicitous misprint. Once, in a typographically more meticulous era, they were infrequent enough to implore the passing tribute of a giggle, but now they come too thick and fast – like, perhaps, the typesetters responsible for them – for me to bother to pick them up, let alone pass them on. Just occasionally, though, an example pops up of such resonant surreality that not to share it would be unforgivably selfish.

I receive a quarterly newsletter from Bay Area Bookmart, a bibliomaniac sales operation I have patronised since my graduate days at Berkeley. On Tuesday, their Winter 88 catalogue arrived, packed to the gunwales with arcane goodies. And one outstanding baddie.

Was there ever offered a more deliciously imponderable snip than a clean first edition of Robert Louis Stevenson's *Travels With A Monkey*?

FEBRUARY

Is it the posthumous destiny of all John Browns to have their souls go marching on? Staring at a hundred purple mountains in Old Brompton Road last Monday and being stared back at by a hundred morose Highland cattle, I could not but reflect that, a century on, the ghillie of ghillies was with us aye.

And had much to answer for. Strolling the somewhat gloomy viewing hangar of Christie's South Kensington for a pre-sale scrutiny of their Victorian paintings auction was not unlike occupying the corner seat of a stopping train to Inverness. Every time I looked up, the watery Caledonian sun was still washing the peak of Ben This or Ben That, two bedraggled piebald cows were standing up to their knees in a winding burn, and a glum urchin with a twig was poised to poke them on.

The only items missing from this interminably replicated scene were the thousands of easels with which the glens must at that time have been spectacularly dotted. For between 1870 and 1900 – such was the effect upon bourgeois taste of the ambiguous spell under which the old Queen had fallen – every English painter with a sovereign to blow on a pint of rose madder and a hank of camelhair was vaulting Hadrian's Wall in the frantic attempt to slap Highland sunsets on to canvas as rapidly and as commercially as possible. Scottish landscape painting was the lucrative tryst at which the Romantic Movement finally embraced the Industrial Revolution.

Which was a pity. As I ambled the long perimeter of Christie's walls with their groaning tonnage of alp and heifer, I could not but be impressed by the remarkable competence of the myriad hands responsible. Had Albert lived to a ripe old age, and the sporran thus never exercised its fateful thrall, who knows to what more creatively fruitful ends all those talented brushes might have twitched?

I had gone to Christie's to examine, and consider bidding for, one of the sale's few pictures of an honest English scene, Charles H. Passey's *A Cornfield With Reapers*. I realize I have written that as if Charles H. Passey were a household name, but as I do not even know what the H. stands for and nor, as far as my researches have gone, does anybody else, you will appreciate that his talent is not one to excite the waving ballpoints of the international wolfpack. Public subscriptions do not have to be raised to stop Passeys emigrating to Tokyo or Des Moines. He does stooks rather well, though, and his kerchiefed yeomen were a jolly brace, and the sky was full of the mellow sunlight that I can get into my living room only by hanging it from a nail, so all in all I reckoned that the Christie's catalogue estimate of around £90 per sq ft was a reasonable price to pay for livening my premises up a bit.

Especially as the thronging dealers which would form my principal competition seemed to be showing scant interest in it. Most of the craning and peering and lip-pulling seemed to be directed at things Scottish – Americans claiming Caledonian provenance, I understand, are prepared to dig deep for such items, particularly (at a guess) if the glum urchin has the family nose – and, with a bit of luck, I might well find myself with a snip over the mantelpiece.

It was even as I was relishing this prospect and beginning, in my head, to rearrange the furniture so that the *cognoscenti*, clapping eyes on the cornfield for the first time, would be able to fall back in stunned admiration without hurting themselves, that a dark shadow fell, as metaphorically as literally, across the waving wheat.

'That's all right, that,' said a soft Hibernian voice, obviously to itself. I turned, to be faced with the largest navy overcoat I had ever seen. Poking from the top of it was the stubbled head of Bob Geldof. He stood back, and considered. He leaned forward, and scanned.

This was bad news. I may not know much about the music business, but, not to put too fine a pun on it, I know that Mr Geldof has more than a bob to his name, and if he had taken a shine to Charles H. Passey, then my wallet was in for a fight it was unlikely to win.

And so, sadly, it proved. I returned on the morrow, took my seat beneath the pulpit well before what was to become a large crowd gathered, and sat for a tremulous hour while various bits of Scotland came and went under the hammer; but when Lot 117 at last came up, though I plunged in and gesticulated like the plucky little optimist I am, I could not stay the course. Considerable interest, as the jargon has it, was shown, the auctioneer's trim head darting this way and that in the manner of a suave robin's, and the cornfield was eventually harvested for £3,200, three times its estimate and my own derisory ceiling.

The battle was fought behind me between dealers I could not see, and I have been unable to ascertain whether they were nodding on their own behalf or on retainer, but, as Queen Victoria probably learned to say, I ha'e me doots. Though Mr Geldof was not this time present in person, I remain convinced that should the snatched masterpiece reappear in an auctioneer's catalogue – when, perhaps, some new aesthetic whim has taken its owner's fancy – it will be yet more seductively described as 'A Cornfield With Reapers, Charles H. Passey, fl 1860-1890, formerly the property of a Boomtown Rat.'

Next day a neighbour telephoned to say that a goldfish was swimming across my lawn. I looked out, in the middle of Wednesday's cyclone, and saw that he was right. My small pond having overflowed into the choppy lake which the garden had become, a couple of midget carp had taken it on the lam and were now striking out for the Baltic, with which Cricklewood was apparently on the point of being seamlessly connected.

Necessity is the mother of chaos. Although Izaak Walton has little to say on the manner of catching fish in a colander, I grabbed this against the option of a saucepan, partly because holes would make trawling easier, partly because God alone knew what trauma might afflict a fish suddenly discovering itself walled in with Teflon and clearly bound for the griddle.

What I had not anticipated was that an implement can have either holes or water in it, but not both. Having, after a pleasant enough ten minutes wading this way and that across the vanished verdure, managed to catch one fugitive, I twigged that to catch the other, the first would have to leap about waterless. As I ran, it somersaulted before me like an Olney pancake.

Nor would you believe the lack of co-operation its colleague brought to its succour. Fifteen further minutes were to pass before – with the two encolandered fish now engaged in battering one another senseless – I could splash back into the house. Where my son, who had selflessly watched all this from the window, peered into the colander and said: 'Those aren't ours.' They are in a basin even as I type. Whose are they? Where are ours?

I blame the Met Office. Why is this country always caught unprepared? Had Ian McCaskill had the foresight to gum a few monitory minnows to his map the night before, all this could have been avoided.

Still, and fenny risk notwithstanding, off to Cambridge on the morrow morn, ploughing up the M11 waterway in the teeth of a Chestertonian gale, the bonnet shipping green, and storm-disorientated gulls wheeling over my wake in hope of jetsam.

The reason behind the crackpot pilgrimage is, of course, obvious. I am going in search of satirical crockery.

The previous evening, knackered by the day's coarse fishing and my equanimity taut, I had allowed myself to engage in an acrimonious barney with a singularly pompous obstetrician who insisted that the first Siamese twins recorded in Britain were Chang and Eng, born in 1814. Whereas I swore that one pair, at least, had been delivered in the 17th century. Had I not, 20 years before, seen them on a plate?

He asked, scoffing, for proof. Not having the plate about me, I was forced to accede to the consensus that I was not a household name where gynaecologists forgathered, and shut up. Nothing else for it, then. My cheeks still burning from the injustice of it all, I hurled myself a dozen hours later into the Fitzwilliam museum, and yes, still there, two decades on, was the plate: two foxy crooks in wigs, holding between them a pitiful infant brace, joined at the chest and identified as 'Prisila & Aquila', with, around the rim, the legend *Behould too persons that are reconsild to rob the parents and to keep the child* . . . It was dated 1680.

The catalogue explained that 'Captain Henry Walrond and Sir Edward Phillips removed the twins from their Somerset parents and made money from displaying them to the public'. I bore you with this personal triumph only because there is no way of proving it to my opponent, other than to publish it. This is because, on inquiry, I discovered that the catalogue I wanted to bear triumphantly to London cost £135. Walrond and Phillips would be proud.

Mr Kenneth Clarke may rant until he is blue enough in the face to have his GP put him out to cardiological tender, but he will never convince me that his White Paper is 'the most formidable programme of reform in the history of the NHS'. I have combed it twice, and it has not one single word to say on the sniper-patient relationship.

Last Friday, I popped in to see a friend recovering in the private Cromwell Hospital from an operation serious enough to warrant two television sets, a three-piece suite in cream antelope hide, gold taps in the vaulted bathroom, and a carpet that swallowed the visiting shin; of none of which, sadly, the patient could take advantage, since she was at the time allowed nothing livelier than a supine suck at a right-angled straw. All money down the drain, you and Robin Cook will doubtless cry, but not a bit of it: had my friend not gone privately, anyone with a telescopic sight could, from the serried roofs opposite, have plugged her where she helpless lay.

I discovered this from her doctor, who had probably dropped

in to see how her current account was getting on. During the course of a chat which, had my car not been on short-term meter, might well have led up to a discreet inquiry as to whether I really needed both kidneys, the doctor revealed that not only were the Cromwell's windows made from bullet-proof glass, but that its high-security suites across the corridor, much used by sickly emirs and the like, had been built to withstand a rocket attack.

When will we be able to get such essentials on the NHS, Mr Clarke? Verily we are two nations, and no mistake.

Which brings me to Archer's Cheese Syndrome. I have just this very day finished the last crumb of the 3lb Cheddar which Jeffrey Archer sends to a hundred selected victims every Christmas. Now, far be it from me to gibe at generosity of so succulent an order, especially as the cheese is built by none other than Grandmaster Alvis – an artist to whom even Mr William Waldegrave's illustrious cheesemaking family defers as Somerset's greatest – but, not to put too fine a point on it, what I get from Jeffrey every Christmas is a cholesterol brick.

Nobody else at home will touch it: they will not even stay in the same room with it, lest their arteries being furring up. It is thus left to me to slice off 2 oz a day and embrace a risk which the great wordsmith has no business at all to make me run. What a pity Jeffrey is not still an MP! He could be hauled before a select committee, like the no less distinguished Edwina, and made to account for his part in the great Cheddar threat to national wind and limb.

They might even manage to stop him publishing his next book.

As a leading amateur practitioner, I cannot over-emphasize the relief I experienced last Saturday at coming upon a man talking to himself in Cricklewood Lane.

It may be helpful here to set a little of the scene, since for those readers unfamiliar with NW2 the words Cricklewood Lane might not only evoke a fetching image of some sylvan glade, but thereby also suggest a simultaneous explanation of why this chap was rabbiting on, viz., he was a poet who, suddenly stumbling upon a host of golden crickles, had begun burbling aloud in the way that poets will. The mundane truth is that Cricklewood Lane is a teeming urban conduit hemmed by seedy Vicwardian brickery, where the only literary composition on offer comes out of an aerosol quill and makes passing stokers blench.

It was here, foursquare on the littered paving between The Friendly Baker and A. A. Baines Turf Accountant, that he stood, last Saturday noon, and turned his private tropes. As he delivered a monologue both trimly articulated and reasonably argued, he appeared neither tight nor barmy; rather, he gave the impression of carrying on a conversation with an old friend who had unaccountably become invisible.

He was perhaps 60, well turned out, and, as I learned while I slowly tied an eavesdropping shoelace beside him, something of an authority on the Vauxhall Cavalier. It was a car which also made him, from time to time, chuckle.

The reason I was relieved was that I had not heard anyone talking to himself in the street for several years. I feared it had died out. When I was young, every other person I passed seemed to be nattering about something, and I'm sure it was good for them to get it off their chests. These days, people tend to bottle things up far too much, which doubtless accounts for the unsettlingly huge increases in stress-related diseases we hear so much about. I should have thought this was an issue crying out for a bit of White Paperwork; but once again, scrutiny proved me wrong.

A last medical shock from this week's casebook.

Yesterday, I happened to read that, in answer to a Commons question, the Social Security Minister Mr Nicholas Scott replied that between 1984 and 1988 the number of centenarian men in Britain had gone up from 100 to 210. According to my pocket calculator, if this alarming trend continues, in a mere 66 years' time the entire male population of this country will be over 100.

Nothing about that in the White Paper, either.

M y first thought was: Methodists have broken in: we have been vandalized by Wesleyans. Thus the ugly mathematics of prejudice: put two and two together and

113

make trouble. It is Monday. Dawn, the colour of a herring's belly, breaks grudgingly over Cricklewood. A man creaks from his bedroom on to his landing, glances automatically from the landing window at a white lawn from which the cryogenised crocuses poke like ice-lollies, starts to go downstairs with this familiar picture held in his waking brain, then, three steps lower, stops.

There is something in the familiar picture which is not familiar at all. The man trudges slowly back up the three steps, and looks out again. By the pond, there is a stone heron. It was not there the day before. And inside the man, bigotry – willy-nilly – works its wormy way.

In fact, his instant prejudice is not directed against the Methodists, but against students. It is simply that (a) the only students in the immediate neighbourhood are Methodist seminarians who share a lodging house a street or so away; that (b) the only citizens likely to nick a stone heron from one place and shin over a wall to put it in another are students; and that (c) the logic of bigotry relies heavily upon undistributed middles.

Never mind that Methodists are not exactly a byword for revelry by night. The man just happens to know that 1989 is the 250th anniversary of the foundation of Methodism, and – since this is just about the only thing he knows about Methodism – he cannot be certain that somewhere within their teetotal canon there is not a footnote to the effect that once every quarter-millennium, disciples are allowed to go on a bit of a commemorative bender.

So the man grinds his teeth, fills his head with the myriad problems of what he should do with a kidnapped sculpture whose anonymous and distraught owners must even now be keening among their deserted gnomes and penguins, unlocks the back door, and pads out grimly into the frost. As the back door slams, the heron *turns its head and looks at him*. Whereupon the man (who knows even less about herons than he knows about Methodists) considers its big beak and the obvious territorial tenacity of its unshifting feet, and goes back inside.

Two hours later, the heron is still there. So, *pace* Esther Rantzen, I telephone the Zoo.

'The heronry,' says the Zoo, 'comes within the remit of the

Regent's Park Superintendent. You will find him on 486 7905.'

'I didn't know you had a heronry,' I say to the Superintendent.

'You can't miss it,' the Superintendent replies. 'It's on Heron Island.'

'Ah. Well, I believe I may have one of your herons,' I tell him.

'You want the Birdman,' says the Superintendent.

Burt Lancaster materializes, inevitably, in my listening head. Is Heron Island a Nash analogue of Alcatraz? A cream-stuccoed Regency chokey, a maximum security villa from which none has ever successfully swum? It transpires not.

'It would normally be Mr Duckett,' continues the Superintendent, 'but Mr Duckett is on holiday.' It's amazing the insights you can be granted into other people's lives. 'Let me put you on to his assistant.'

'Are you a heron short?' I ask Mr Duckett's assistant.

'Where are you?'

'A couple of miles away. It's by my pond.'

'It would be,' says the assistant. 'They are foraging a bit. Feeding up, due to the start of the breeding season. You've probably noticed its plumage is pinker than normal.'

'Er, now you mention it,' I say, as one ever on the *qui vive* for the slightest tell-tale change in feather hue.

'Yes, everything's on the move. We've got cormorants on the lake this morning.'

'Astonishing,' I say, since it sounds as though it might be.

'Your pond, does it have fish in it?'

'It did yesterday.'

'Exactly my point,' says the assistant. 'Just walk slowly up to it and clap your hands. It'll go quietly.'

'Will it come back?'

'Quite possibly. They're very territorial. The thing is, just *because* they're very territorial and they won't encroach on another one's patch, there's one fairly certain method of keeping them away.'

'Which is?'

'Get a stone heron,' says Mr Duckett's assistant, 'and put it by the pond.'

I cannot of course speak for mice, but whatever the shortcomings of man's best-laid plans, they nevertheless have a thick edge over his worst.

On Monday afternoon, I bought another car. The first car I bought on Monday, I bought in the morning. Since, however, it could not be delivered until mid-April – a fact I did not know when I divested myself of my previous car last Friday – I realized some two hundred pedestrian yards after I had bought it that I needed something to get me from A to B, i.e., February to April. The stout-booted among you may question the use of *needed* there, but for someone who, since he threw away his L-plates in 1956, has been used to travelling by chair, eight weeks is an unconscionable time.

Back home at last, exhausted, I could net nothing cheaper from my broken-winded phone trawl of rental companies than £1,000 for the two-month period. On the other hand, it would have been evident to the merest clod that to buy a car for anything less than that amount and then sell it again in April made immeasurably better sense. Which may explain why the merest clods have such a tough time of it in this world.

By 2.30pm, I had wrenched it from the unwilling hands of an extremely nice man who had made the mistake of advertising it in our local paper, doubtless hoping against hope that no one would believe you could buy a 1971 Austin 1100 for only £295, and he would thus be able to spend the rest of his life with the car he loved. No such luck: the truth – which in his innocence he couldn't possibly have known – is that a buyer of such a car is actually born every minute.

I pressed the folding money on him, and left him weeping. Call me brute, but there are winners and losers in this life, and that is the way it is. Just to test his theory that if he had only had the time to clean it up a bit it would have been worth every penny of £500, I took it, on my lurching way home, through the Fortune Green car wash.

The wing fell off.

Metro Breakers Ltd is tucked away below the A41 in Colin Deep Lane. It is impossible to get to unless you have a car, so I counted myself enormously fortunate in having one to go and get a wing for it in; even if the story does play hell with one's syntax. I had been put on to Metro Breakers Ltd by the man who runs the car wash. I left him my old wing in gratitude: someday, he may need something to tell his grandchildren.

I fear my style is scant match for Metro Breakers Ltd. You'd need Dante. Not only is *Lasciate ogni speranza voi ch'entrate!* the first cry to spring to one's lips on passing through its dreadful gate, but in abandoning that hope you realize that where you are doing it is almost certainly *nel mezzo del cammin di nostra vita* of which he spake. Thousands of bereft motorists fetch up here, poking about among the mountainous piles of busted cars in vain quest of a suitable crankshaft, an apt door, a consonant clutch housing, or, indeed, a 1971 offside wing for an Austin 1100, praying that the right bit will turn up and that they can quickly get back onto whatever remains of life's dwindling road.

It is a grim spectacle and a grimmer game, this endless clambering over piles of dismembered bits. It contains more than a hint of what might happen should the trade in kidney transplanting get out of hand.

But I did not, though I scaled two teetering alps of mudguards, find an unrusted 1100 wing. In the rude camaraderie of purgatory, however, I struck up a brief acquaintance with a man in fruitless search of an MGA boot-lid, who knew a place in Kingsbury where they broke 1100s for paying cannibals.

It cost me £40, primed and ready for paint.

The man behind the Universal Auto Spares (Colindale) paint-counter pursed a professional lip.

'There's aubergine,' he said, 'and aubergine.'

'Even in 1971?' I said.

'*Particularly* in 1971,' he said. There came into his eyes that low yet fierce light which invariably indicates that a bee is at work in the bonnet above. 'I have often wondered what got into manufacturers in 1971. It is no exaggeration to say the colour charts went mad. Nine different olives, as I recall.'

'How many aubergines?'

'Five, at least,' he said. 'Could be six.'

'It's an Austin 1100,' I said, 'if that's any help.'

'Not much,' he said. 'BL aubergine was a bugger for blooming. It was what we call fugitive. Whatever it was in 1971, it won't be now. Could very well be purple. 'Or,' he added darkly, 'worse.'

'The car's outside,' I said. 'Perhaps you . . .'

He walked all round it.

'It's got three different aubergines on, for a start,' he said. 'Been in a lot of bangs, has it?'

'I don't know,' I said. 'I've just bought it.'

He looked at me.

'Closest we come is aconite,' he said, finally. 'It won't match, but so what? You could tell people it's four aubergines.'

I could, but I don't. I tell them it's rented.

Any minute, mind, none of this will be of the slightest consequence to me. I shall be lying off Tahiti waiting for dusky nubilia to swim out to my nuclear yacht and stuff kumquats in my mouth. That is the kind of thing we millionaires do. Even Deutschmark millionaires.

Quite why the German economy should need 72 quid from me to shore it up I cannot begin to guess, but the Fatherland has written to me to say that if I can see my way clear to coughing up this short-term loan, it will send me one million Deutschmarks by March 25. Almost certainly. As the accompanying glossy folder exhorts, with an engaging Teuton lilt: 'If you do not yet hold a stake in the Northwest German State Lottery, it is high time to become acquainted with Lady Luck!'

I have always been baffled by the subscription lists I appear to be on. The rest of my family receives relatively sensible offers about share flotations, complete sets of Trollope in handsome vellumetto, and free test drives of Volvos. Last week, I was invited to join the Houston Cookie Club and enjoy a genuine Down Home fruit cake every month in a choice of 50 flavours, flown direct from Texas. This week, Germany is standing on the mat with its hand out.

They have also sent a photograph of one million

Deutschmarks, so that when the stuff arrives I shall be able to identify it. It is just a matter of course. Naturally, I shall have to learn the German for 'This will not change my life, I shall be down the pit tomorrow as usual,' and steel myself for the kiss of an unknown Hanseatic starlet, but it's worth it. Never look a gift horse in the mouth is my motto.

Even when *Gift* means poison.

MARCH

Some days, a coincidence can make the heart bound. If you are very lucky, the coincidence may strike a keynote for the day. Or unlucky.

Last Friday was my daughter's half term; we decided to meet for tea and see the film of *Alice in Wonderland*. Now, since my daughter is 16, and since all her foxy friends, upon reading the previous sentence, will immediately begin smacking their foreheads, rolling their eyes, and making regurgitant gestures, let me attempt to extenuate derision by pointing out that the *Alice* in question owes nothing to Disney (and little enough to Lewis Carroll), being instead Jan Svankmajer's grotesque expressionist re-interpretation at the ICA, fashionably Czech, hamfistedly Freudian, and horribly adult.

Furthermore, tea was to be at the Ritz, long the venue of the classy tryst, where I was hoping to pass my daughter off as my mistress and see what the gossip columns might subsequently come up with in the way of tax-free out-of-court settlements.

I hove to at 3.45, nattily suited, suede-shod, and sporting my new Lock fedora, believing that I should thereby harmonize with the Ritz's archaically romantic environment, in reasonable pastiche of Rex Harrison. That this effect was immediately squelched was due in no small measure to Rex Harrison, who, hardly had I stationed myself in the lobby, came through the swing doors in an even sleeker fedora, and, like an era passing, crept softly to the lift. I felt my hat wilt.

Two minutes later, my daughter arrived, in a green trilby. But no sooner had this bizarre hatmotif begun to thread itself through the afternoon's footnotes than it sprang suddenly into the main text. Approaching the head waiter, I asked him to show us to a table for tea.

He said: 'I'm afraid there isn't any room'. We peered past him.

'There's *plenty* of room!' cried Victoria, not ungleefully. The Mad Hatter looked at her.

'Those tables are booked, madam,' he said. 'May I suggest Fortnum's?'

'Let's all move one place on, eh?' murmured Victoria. As Carroll elsewhere wrote, they were all of them fond of quotations.

The sixth floor at Fortnum's remains locked, not in the Ritz's *belle époque*, but in 1946. The décor is High Attlee. Nippies in black bombazine and white pinafores twinkle hither and yon. A pianist prises Vivian Ellis from a boudoir grand. If there is trysting afoot, it is impeccably covert. Rex Harrison never set brogue in the place. It is just possible that Trevor Howard once met Celia Johnson here, but very briefly, even for them.

I was halfway through my second crumpet and a fascinating lecture on the tearooms of yesteryear, which had glazed my daughter's eyes by the second sentence, when I suddenly noticed those eyes wake, and swivel upwards.

'Excuse me,' said a voice above my right shoulder. I looked up, into the face of an elegant citizen in a check jacket, and a doe-skin waistcoat. The waistcoat had a watch-chain across it. He had a red carnation in his buttonhole too, but the watch-chain was the clincher. I knew immediately why Victoria's jaw had dropped.

'Do forgive the intrusion, Mr Coren,' said the White Rabbit, 'but would you sign a book for me?'

'Of course,' I said. I reached out a hand, praying that its tremble would not betray its eagerness. The White Rabbit, however, stepped a pace back.

'I haven't got the book yet,' he said. 'I thought I'd nip next door to Hatchard's and buy one, if you could bear to wait a tick.'

'We do have to be at the ICA by five,' I said, 'but of course . . .'

It was at this point that the White Rabbit actually *took a watch out of his waistcoat pocket*. The italics are Carroll's.

'I'll be back in a jiffy,' he said, and dashed out. Five minutes passed.

'Ha!' said Victoria. 'Bet Hatchard's didn't have one. Bet he's too nice to come back and tell you. Either that, or he was winding you up.'

'Rubbish!' I cried. 'Come on.'

The Fortnum's lift is the slowest in London. 'Down, down, down,' murmured Victoria, 'would the fall *never* come to an end?'

We sprinted along Piccadilly, and into Hatchard's.

'Look,' I said to an assistant, 'embarrassing question, but did a big chap in a check jacket . . .'

'Red carnation? Yes, but I'm afraid we didn't have a hardback, I sent him downstairs to paperbacks.'

We took the stairs three at a time, holding onto our hats. 'Red carnation? Yes, he just bought a paperback, shall I see if . . .?'

It was too late to stop her. She led the chase. We lapped the basement, leapt the stairs.

'He just went past me,' cried the hardback lady, 'into the street.'

We were just in time to see, through 50 yards of gloaming, the White Rabbit sprint into Fortnum's.

'We'll miss the film,' warned my daughter.

'Oh God,' I moaned. 'What'll he think of me?'

We turned towards the ICA.

'Life, what is it but a nightmare?' said Victoria.

On Sunday, the house depth-charges me awake at 7am. It is a solid enough house, but the door-knocker far below is being banged with such vigour that I have been blasted from sleep not by noise but by concussion.

What can it be but grim news? This is a copper's knock. Having hit the pit before the children returned last night, and thus having no proof that they have returned at all, I age considerably on the downstairs canter. There will be two Old Bills on the steps, ensobering their faces as laid down in the Hendon College guidelines: word will have arrived from Newport Pagnell that my son, last seen jogging at dusk on Finchley Road, has been prised out of a juggernaut's treads; a phone call from the Marseilles nick will have confirmed that my daughter, unable to face the ordeal of GCSE, arrived on the midnight flight and joined the French Foreign ATS ...

What is on the step is not two burly ruddy-cheeked men in blue but one small olive man in a kaftan. He holds a black bin-liner in one hand, and a suitcase in the other. There is about him a distinctly furtive air, and I do not altogether reject the possibility that he belongs to a culture where female adultery is still taken seriously and dealt with accordingly, that his wife is therefore either in the bin-liner or the suitcase (or perhaps both), and that, knowing me to be a hack, he wishes me to represent his shaky case in the public prints.

Before I can speak, he reaches into the bin-liner, but, instead of a foot or a lung, what comes out is a bunch of daffodils.

'For Mother's Day,' he explains – if, since I am not his mother, you can call it explanation. He then opens the suitcase, which is full of soap and Black Magic.

I do not, though, bust him in the mouth. How can I, given my political persuasion? The chap has identified a gap in the market. He is an exemplar of the enterprise culture. He has got on his bike. On this, her day of days, surely the Great Mother Of Us All would wholeheartedly approve?

Whether she, however, turfed out of her Downing Street sack with the moon still up, would meekly have purchased a fistful of flaccid daffodils and wimped back inside, I beg leave to question.

On the morning of M-Day+1, irony's mischievous hand dumps me in the basement of LBC, whither Brian Hayes has invited me to co-host his astringent phone-in. Hermetically sealed into the two-man cubicle and connected to one another only by earphones, I suddenly fancy, so clenched is my jaw and so arrythmic my pulse, that we are not beneath Gough Square at all, we are ten thousand feet up over the Ruhr, coaxing a stricken

Lancaster back to Stradishall, the tailplane in ribbons and the odds on a fried breakfast growing longer by the minute.

In the event, and despite the Skipper's canny hand, the flight was indeed pretty rocky. The irony adumbrated above was ITV's, who chose Mother's Night to transmit *Place of Safety*, a harrowing dramatization of a child-abuse case, uncoincidentally set in Cleveland; and although Brian had earlier assured me that callers would address a wide variety of topics, some of which might merit the frivolous attention for which I had been drafted, nobody, on the morning after, wanted to talk about anything but assaults on children.

I spent a bad hour. It was simple enough at the start to muster glib generalizations about medical zealots, crass bureaucrats, inept procedures, under-funded services, and so on: tabloid pontification isn't difficult, ask any barman. It was when the calls started to come in, not from non-combatant wafflers but from actual victims and perpetrators, that inadequacy furred my tongue. Your straits must be pretty dire if you have no one to turn to but a couple of unqualified voices dovetailing their responses between chirpy commercials and traffic bulletins, and as the fraught confessions stuttered through the head-set, I could find nothing to offer them.

Somehow, the Skipper got us down in one piece. His notorious acerbity masks, perhaps protects, a great depth of humanity and understanding, and I doff my helmet to him. I shall, however, send him a copy of Nathanael West's *Miss Lonelyhearts*, as a warning of what can happen to you if you stay out there too long.

Walking back home, I paused in the tiny Paddington Street parklet laid over the site, a plaque says, of the garret occupied in 1790 by Le Vicomte de Chateaubriand. It doesn't say what he was doing in the garret – he could have been working on his recipe for steak, perhaps – but I was suddenly snatched out of this highly profitable line of wool-gathering by a most curious incident.

Well, curious to me, but if I know *Times* correspondents and their ornithomantic little ways, someone is bound to write to me with a smart gloss on the text. Which is that, as I sat there, a tabby cat quietly sleeping on a wonky urn opposite was suddenly startled by a pigeon. The pigeon came in low, jabbed its beak at the cat's head as it overflew, missed, climbed like an Me 109, turned, and came back out of the trees for a second pass. This time, with the woken cat frenziedly punching the air, the pigeon landed some kind of hit; the cat fled.

Explanations, please, on a postcard.

Since there is perhaps nothing more worrying than worrying about what it is you ought to be worrying about, it is high time that the Junior Minister for Klaxons issued a pamphlet clearly identifying the myriad sources of things that go whoop in the night.

There is that penetrating bray which is not unlike the sound you would expect were a mule to take up the cornet (if that is the kind of thing you are given to expecting); then there is its obverse (haw-hee); there is the siren undulation adopted from American *films noirs*; there is the shrill hoop-hoop-hoop which suggests that the Armilla Patrol is steaming up Finchley Road in line astern; there is the high-pitched tinny whine which tails away to a sort of resigned croak; and there are all sorts of bells.

That these variously denote that the police, the fire brigade, Special Branch, the ambulance service, the SPG, the Bomb Squad, and umpteen other mobile altruists are hurtling hither and yon through the caring society is not enough, when you are lying awake at 3am. You need to be able to assess the level of trembling required: is this merely a domestic barney in Kilburn, or is something fanning rapidly outwards from Pudding Lane? Are *fedayeen* parachutists plummeting towards Penguin Books, or is it just the Swiss Cottage contraflow again? Should we, in short, pull the duvet over our heads, or start bunging our travel requisites into a carpet-bag?

The problem is even more acute when it happens away from home; even if you have somehow discovered what the assorted noises signify in London, that doesn't mean that they use the same phonophores in wooded Hampshire.

Around Monday midnight, I was awoken in the guest bedroom

of a New Forest cottage by all this stuff going off at once. Clearly, every emergency service in the south-east was homing in on some single cataclysm; and since it is my belief, Watson, that the lowest and vilest alleys of London do not present a more dreadful record of sin than does the smiling and beautiful countryside, I was out of my bunk in a trice and frantically tugging apart the Laura Ashleys.

Beyond lay a heart-stopping sight. The whole stretch of heathland west of Cadnam was lit by eerie polychrome flashes; the sky was full of weird iridescent blips. You will appreciate that it was not difficult for the febrile imagination to connect these mysteries with the siren sounds and come to extremely unsettling conclusions: this was either a highly ambitious open-air production of *King Lear*, or else something truly ghastly was up. Did all these wailing alarms perhaps belong to the hitherto unpublicized Ozone Layer Squad? Had Porton Down gone critical? Had George Bush managed to wangle a yet more convivial candidate than John Tower into the defence turret and was he even now stumbling drunkenly from button to button as if there were, quite literally, no tomorrow?

A rock in a crisis, I was about to pad across the landing and gently rouse the other guests with some such sturdy reassurance as 'THE SKY IS FALLING! THE SKY IS FALLING!' when my own door suddenly opened and the livid light identified my host, just quickly enough to thwart cardiac arrest. After all – flashing welkin, howling sirens, panic in the streets – could anyone blame me for expecting a triffid?'

'Glad you're still up,' he said. 'Be a pity to miss the aurora borealis.'

Town mice learn to be quick on their feet, if they wish to escape the bucolic derision that is ever on the *qui vive* to entrap them.

'Yes,' I said, 'it's really not bad at all, for England. I remember once, mind, up in Stavanger, I . . .'

I thought it wisest, since he seemed to have paid no attention to them, not to mention the sirens. They would only turn out to belong to the Special Poaching Group or the Dutch Elm Brigade or some such impenetrable rural enigma.

Which brings me to the Feral Tomato. This is not some lissom indiscretion from Mr Tower's past, but exactly what it sounds like, unfortunately. Another Forest guest was a hot-shot geneticist who tinkers with the chromosomes of vegetables so that they do what the food industry wants. His current ambition being the ultimate potato, he had recently attended an EEC conference on veggie DNA, where the life had been frightened out of him by a Belgian whose learned paper let drop the confession that he had developed a tomato which had gone out of control.

The fact is, the guest explained (somewhat smugly, I thought), that whereas a potato is as sexually inert as a vegetable can be, the tomato is exactly other. It needs very little prompting to get up to things which, *mutatis mutandis*, would get it three years in Parkhurst. And *mutatis mutandis* was precisely the issue – the Belgian had so interfered with the tame tomato as to render it feral. Not only was it inter-pollinating to produce giant offspring, it was likely to cross-pollinate spontaneously with anything that so much as glanced at it.

'The mutant possibilities,' murmured our geneticist, 'are virtually incalculable.'

The next time there are lights in the sky, lock the door. It could be The Day of the Tomatoes.

A s I'm sure you have heard, there is a willow grows aslant a brook; but this need be no cause for freehold alarm. Its owner may rest easy in his bed. He has infringed nothing. Even in as rotten a state as Denmark, council officials with raised umbrellas do not go ambling along brooks.

And should someone be daft enough to clamber the pendent bough in order to hang thereon her coronet weeds, and as the result wind up starring in her own inquest, the tree's owner may confidently point out to the Elsinore coroner that the deceased was barking mad. Anyone could tell this from the way she was singing as she floated off; whereupon contributory negligence will be recorded in the ledger, and the owner walk scot-free. Moreover, the owner will, if he has a smart lawyer, be able to sue the deceased's estate on the grounds that she broke an envious sliver off his tree, and these things cost money.

Where an arbutus grows aslant the road, however, it is an entirely different kettle of legislation.

Two flourishing examples of this hapless breed stand sentinel at either corner of my front garden, bursting annually into both creamy blossom and those fine fat scarlet fruit which look remarkably like strawberries but taste depressingly like rancid swede; a literally bitter disappointment which jays – who are clearly slow learners – express by spitting them on to the car.

I do not, however, take the jays to court. What I take is the rough with the smooth: if the price of having big showy trees is a car splattered with crypto-strawberries, so be it. I do not believe in interfering with nature. That is the major difference between me and the London Borough of Barnet.

For the London Borough of Barnet has just served me with an order requiring me to lop my two arbutus – which admittedly overhang the pavement – on the grounds that passers-by are unable to walk under them. Upon receipt of the order, I immediately went out and walked under them. Though no dwarf, I even went so far as to put my trilby on: there was a foot's clearance.

I went back inside and picked up the phone.

'One of our inspectors,' explained Barnet, 'was impeded when attempting to pass beneath.'

'You have a seven-foot inspector,' I said. 'This strikes me as dirty play.'

'It isn't a question of his height,' said Barnet. 'He had his umbrella up. It was his umbrella which was unable to pass beneath the tree.'

'He could have put his umbrella down and stood under the tree until it stopped,' I said, reasonably. 'It is an evergreen, and thickly foliated.'

'That isn't the point, either,' said Barnet. 'He wasn't just walking about in the rain. He was inspecting trees to ensure that passage was possible with an umbrella raised, as required by the by-laws.'

Are there no depths to which men will not descend in return

for an index-linked pension? What kind of psychopath prowls the landscape with an umbrella for the sole purpose of maiming its finest flora?

'Who is this lout?' I enquired.

'It is not our practice,' began Barnet, 'to reveal the . . .'

'I thought it mightn't be,' I said. A different tack hove into view. 'Perhaps you could at least tell me,' I inquired, 'whether he tripped over much?'

'I don't follow.'

'I just wondered,' I said, 'whether, in the course of this arboreal inspection, he had fallen over any of the broken paving stones I have been attempting to interest you in since about 1980. Many do. Indeed, the risk of having one's umbrella damaged by my trees is considerably reduced by the fact that, by the time they reach my house, most people are on their hands and knees.'

'Is this correspondence on our files?' said Barnet.

'How the hell should I know?'

'There is no need,' said Barnet, 'to get abusive.'

He was, for the first time, right. What there was need to get was a chunk of broken paving stone, stagger round to the council offices with it, and bung it through the front window in the hope of hitting the arboriphobe with the umbrella.

It might, of course, come as no surprise to the skulking umbrella man. These days sudden violence can visit us from the most unlikely and unexpected quarters. I am indebted, for the lurid illustration of this, to Mr Kevin Hempsall of Scunthorpe who has sent me a cutting from the *Police Gazette* of February 17, apropos an October column of mine extolling *la cuisine Perigordine*.

I quote his dreadful gobbet: 'Police in the Dordogne seized and destroyed 40 tonnes of *pâté de foie gras* this week, after several tins of it exploded.'

Thank you, Mr Hempsall. I still have several tins of my own in the fridge, and intend poking them with a long stick. Heaven, *pace* Sydney Smith, may well be eating *pâté de fois gras* to the sound of trumpets, but actually ending up there as the result of eating *pâté* to the sound of detonations is not exactly my idea of it.

The spotlight exacts a heavy toll: falter in it, and its capricious beam will swivel towards the writing on the wall. Today the wall has bad news for Boris: it is time to hang up his plimsolls.

As his countryman Goethe so sagely pointed out, when his famed backhand finally lost its cunning, *Die Tat ist alles, nicht der Ruhm.* In a culture as hero-obsessed as Becker's, Siegfried is always on borrowed time, because Hagen is always out there in the wings, limbering up. Or, in Boris's case, I am.

Germany has written to me. It wants to know how good my tennis is. It wrote, moreover, beneath the letterhead of The Queen's Club, home of the Lawn Tennis Association: an imprimatur impregnable to scrutiny. It seems that the Fatherland has persuaded the game's governing body to set up something entitled the LTA Volkswagen Ratings Computer, and it is this which invited me to submit my game to software eager to determine my playing status. Those who come up to snuff will doubtless be offered German nationality, in the fervent patriotic hope that this year's Wimbledon Ball may be opened by someone trundling Steffi Graf backwards for the twinned glory of the Bundesrepublik.

Very flattering, of course, but also puzzling. How did Volkswagen know I played tennis? Do open Golf convertibles crawl the perimeters of our parks, scouts standing in the back like Erwin Rommel, Zeiss binoculars ever on the qui vive for lob and volley? I fear not. Something . . . call it the way I have of leaning on the net-post, coughing . . . tells me it is not my quality of shot that has commended me, but simply our old friend Big Microchip, who watches our every commercial move, via credit card records. I can think only that some sporting purchase of mine, some piece of leading-edge kit designed to squeeze one more percentage-point out of the seemingly unimprovable game of the truly gifted – a revolutionary new arch-support, perhaps, a quantum leap on the liniment front – has alerted the VWLTA to my potential.

Potential? Not, I think, for international stardom, remunerative endorsements, or, in my honoured sunset, a chain of Mediterranean coaching centres, but for something a mite more

133

mundane. I note from their communication that, if I register, I will not only receive generous discounts on Hertz car rental, RAC membership, selected insurance policies, tennis holidays, and much else besides, I will also automatically enter the Prize Draw for Sergio Tacchini tennis socks, Pro-Kennex tennis racquets, Penn tennis balls, Club Sportif tennis hols in Kenya, and, yes, a VW Golf. Which is probably due for relaunch as the VW Tennis any moment now.

Nor do I doubt that this feisty marketing would end there: what can it be which makes me suspect that membership of the VWLTA would lead to yet more glossy blandishments arriving through my door? Why, once my rank was established on the great computer ('new ratings are listed in the January edition of *Serve and Volley Magazine*'), who knows how many selfless tennis buffs would want to beat a path to my door, offering me unimaginably generous deals on everything from cut-price osteopathy and designer pacemakers to pro-am Zimmer frames and chic memorial urns?

Not tennis, however, but golf (the lower-case variety) was the conversational mainstay of a cheery private – and all-male – lunch to send Denis Thatcher off to Africa in relaxed mood.

I was there, but could not join in. Not simply because I had nothing useful to add concerning dog-leg fifth and goose-neck putter (if, indeed, it wasn't dog-leg putter and goose-neck fifth) but because I had found myself suddenly mesmerized by all the wondrous queries that no one was putting to the great consort, but which nevertheless filled the convivial air, unspoken. The adroitness with which his radiant helpmeet avoids answering questions was as nothing to the efforts made by the company to avoid asking them. Merely mentioning one's own wife's name in passing was enough to plunge the table into excited reminiscences of the tricky 14th at Lytham.

After he had gone, those remaining not surprisingly launched themselves into the vast unasked with huge gusto and invention. I find, fortunately perhaps, that I can remember none of their inquiries, save one, seriously put by a thoughtful and distinguished cove who genuinely wanted to know only whether the Prime Minister rinsed out her own stockings, and, if so, whether she hung them over the shower-spout to dry.

For some unfathomable reason, this shut us up for some time, but whether the majority were thinking about him, or about her, or about us . . . or indeed about Walpole and Attlee . . . was a supplementary which nobody seemed prepared to put.

As incongruity would have it, that same night the American comedian Jackie Mason and I were dinner guests of our shared publisher, Jeremy Robson. That is to say, Jeremy and I had dinner: Mr Mason, unmoved by either the considerable reputation of the restaurant or the chagrin of its staff, ordered only a cup of tea. You can do that, if you're a star. His girl friend ordered only a cup of tea, too. She didn't like it, and sent it back. You can do that if you're a star's girl friend.

G rim news. The street has its first Ambassadorial Residence.

It does not, you understand, have an ambassador *in* residence, merely a residence waiting for an ambassador to come and reside in it, but it can be only a matter of time, if Benham and Reeves have anything to do with it. Their sign appeared yesterday morning, four residences up the road. Indeed, it is quite possible, at so auspicious a moment in Cricklewood's hitherto modest diplomatic history, that the sign was actually put there by Benham and Reeves themselves – Benham holding the pole, perhaps, while Reeves swung the mallet – but that is only romantic surmise. I did not catch them at it, I merely reeled back at the escutcheoned result.

FOR SALE, it said, AMBASSADORIAL RESIDENCE.

Quite how their Nomenclature Department arrived at this designation, who can fathom? To the casual eye, the house is not even Consular. Its closest friends would blush to call it Thirdsecretarial. As a matter of fact, when it last went on the market, four years ago, it was LARGE FAMILY HOME, and that, to some of us, was gilding the lily.

Since then, however, it has been tarted up. It has been

135

diplomatized to the highest standards. Initially a five-bedroomed Edwardian redbrick, it has recently had men in the roof. They have now gone, and left the pre-cast dormers of four new attic bedrooms poking through the tiles, so that the house now has an impressive third storey in the ever-popular dog's-dinner style. It also has a neo-Palladian portico in acropolitan polystyrene – when the truck arrived, I did, for a brief heady moment, think the two columns might be marble, until a tiny bloke hopped off the back with one under each arm – and a sweeping carriage drive, almost big enough for two cars, in a fetching carmine asphalt so robust as to have weathered the current warm spell with hardly a bubble. Oh yes, and it's got a reproduction lamp-post at one end: I have not seen it lit as yet, but even so, you can tell it would look very smart with an ambassador leaning on it.

Which, of course, is the aspect that bothers me most. I have seen ambassadorial residences elsewhere, five stretched black Mercedes immunely stacked on the pavement out front, shirtsleeved constables chatting up giggling chambermaids much in the manner of some lawks-a-mercy ITV costume serial, a couple of dispirited coves in clotted beards parading a hand-lettered sign demanding that the President hang himself, and I have not liked what I have seen.

And those were in such recognizedly ambassadorial districts as Kensington and St Johns Wood, where one may generally assume that the embassies belong to countries you can find on a map. But we are a fair hike, down here, from the Court of St James: what kind of nation is going to dump its plenipotentiary in Cricklewood? If Benham and Reeves see their seductive ways rewarded, we shall end up with His Excellency the Ambassador for Ghastli, granted his portfolio, no doubt, for defenestrating the previous President and prising the green eye of the little yellow god from the hapless crook's Zurich account for the grateful benefit of the incoming megalomaniac.

He will have eight hysterical wives and as many raddled mistresses, he will throw all-night thrashes for his diplomatic sidekicks from Grisli, and Lower Behavia, and The New Peccadilloes, he will park the Ghastlian fleet of clapped-out Morris Oxfords all over the verges, and his ululating bodyguard will sit in the dormer windows plugging our domestic animals with their Uzis, on the unassailable grounds that this is Ghastlian territory, where the cat is known to be the corporeal form of Old Nick.

He will naturally be overthrown every other week, to be immediately underthrown again, with the result that our presently benign air will reek constantly from stun grenades and incinerating files, and echo with the noise of ricochet and disembowelling. No doubt, too, our own plucky Queen's Light Balaclavas will occasionally be called upon to abseil down our wistaria and burst through our bedroom windows in order to set up forward beachheads for bullhorn and mortar and Prime Ministerial walkabout.

I shall probably move, provided Benham's still bother with ordinary English houses. Then again, they could always call it THIS FORMERLY CASTELLAR RESIDENCE.

APRIL

The man says: 'Would you mind telling me what you are doing here?' It is an attempt at the voice of authority, but he is not dressed for authority. He has a grey woollen shirt, a woven red tie, brown corduroy trousers scuffed at the knee and those shoes that look like Cornish pasties. Nor does he have the stance of authority; he is slightly on the back foot, and as I raise my jamjar, he flinches. We are alone, in wooded country, albeit within bus noise, and I can see in his eyes the fearful look of a man imagining headlines. He is thinking: *Lecturer Slain by Jamjar Maniac.*

The last time I was here, at the top of Cat Hill, on the Cockfosters border, was nearly forty years ago. Before the little lake beside which we are both standing was fenced off from the road. I had a jamjar that time too.

'I have a pond,' I reply. 'As a matter of fact, I have two.'

'This lake is the property of Middlesex Polytechnic,' he counters tremulously. Clearly he thinks I am here to steal his lake. He thinks I am a mad pond collector, two at home but still insatiable. He thinks I go out on Good Friday to nick any area of standing water left unguarded through bank holiday insouciance.

'Sorry, sorry, didn't realize it belonged to anyone, haven't been here since I was ten. I used to come here to collect newts.'

'Well, there's no fishing now.' He points to a sign. It says NO FISHING.

141

'I wonder if that applies to newts,' I say. 'It's an interesting point, don't you think?'

'What is?'

God knows what he lectures in. Something modern and mousy. Supply-side semiotics, possibly, crisis theology, that sort of thing. Any day now, Kenneth Baker will peg him out for the ants.

'Whether a newt is a fish within the meaning of the Act,' I explain. 'Whether responsibility devolves upon Middlesex Polytechnic, their heirs and assigns, for not putting up a board saying NO NEWTING.'

'I don't think we have any newts,' he says. He delivers this message like a shop assistant; they might get a delivery on Thursday but he can't promise, you know what it is like with newts, also staff shortages at our Runcorn depot.

'I don't want any newts,' I assure him. 'What I need is frogspawn.'

'Frogspawn?'

'Shouldn't think that infringes anything, would you? *De minimis non curat lex*, eh?'

He takes half a step towards me, and stops. Is he considering whether it is worth laying down his life to save Middlesex Poly's frogspawn? Then he turns, suddenly, and runs away.

I splosh into the shallows, but there is no spawn where there used to be spawn. Nor are there mobs of cheery piggybacking frogs gummed together in annual ecstasy, the way there were on ancient Easters.

Why? I suspect that Middlesex Polytechnic is up to something in the Cat Hill pond, weed engineering, scum warfare; this is not unlike Part One of some doomy low-lit vertiginously shot TV serial in which a decent type Stumbles Onto Something. Any minute now my car will blow up.

I glance up from these musings at a shout. The lecturer is loping back through the trees. He has two large henchmen with him. I take it on the lam. I should stay and ask them what the thirty-nine steps are, but it is years since I used a jamjar at close quarters.

It is the clement winter which has thrown my ponds out of joint. Hitherto, it has been the practice of my frogs, around December, to stick their metabolism in neutral, take a last deep breath, and burrow into the insulating mulch for their hibernal kip, setting their sexual alarms for March.

This winter they have been out and about. Puzzled as to where the flies go in the wintertime, they have been wandering far from base in search of food and have clearly hopped it into so remote a diaspora as to have forgotten where they habitually return for a bit of the vernal other.

Thus I need to seed the pond, and thus Cat Hill. Where else would a middle-aged spawn-fancier go but back to the hunting-grounds of his childhood? After the age of ten, one meets no new ponds. There was another, I recall as I drive hurriedly away, on nearby Hadley Common – and yes, despite a rich interim burgeoning of executive homesteads, it is still there! Its strand teems encouragingly with small muddy boys: nothing has changed since VE-Day.

And there is spawn, not merely wobbly chunks of common frog but also the frail linear ectoplasm of the toad, and I fill my jar and drive home gingerly, my foster-embryos wedged between my thighs, and decant them into a bucket, where they will stay until legged and nippy enough to stand an even chance in the predatory pondwaters.

The house is quiet. The children are at Hampstead Fair for the evening . . .

Having gone out to dinner, I did not see them until Saturday morning. They had a good time. They won five goldfish and three coconuts. They swapped the coconuts for three more goldfish. They thank me for my faith in their accuracy with dart and hoop. Fancy leaving a bucket there! A chill strikes my heart.

The goldfish would thank me even more for my consideration in having a tin bucket ready, if they could. It is not every day that street-urchin tiddlers get brought home to a slap-up caviare supper.

One Grand Prix may not make a summer, but it can go a long way towards boosting the eternal hopes of spring. I bring cheering news for our aspirant world champion. After Brazil, he is clearly a household word, even among the most grudgingly unpartisan race in the world. *Un mot de ménage*, as we say here in Provence.

Late last Sunday afternoon, hurtling from Cannes towards Monte Carlo at a speed reflecting the dangerous seductions with which two such resonant names may lure the susceptible, I glanced into my rear-view mirror to find it filled with more than golden sunset. Two alien moustaches appeared to be sitting on my back seat. I was being slipstreamed, at something over 100 mph, by a black Porsche. It had a French number plate. Ever mindful of the complex international incumbencies under which Mrs Thatcher has placed us all, I loyally shoved my shoe as far as it would go into the engine compartment, and squeezed a few further revs out of the howling crankshaft.

Whereupon the Porsche opened its headlight flaps and shot a couple of yellow blinks, not unlike a panther giving notice of lunch; so I pulled over, and it growled past me at around 120, offering in derisive farewell that faint puff of exhaust which betokens a swine who has several gears to change he hasn't even unpacked yet.

But on vernal Sunday evenings, the A8 autoroute is a busy strip. When, a couple of kilometres further on, the Monte Carlo *péage* loomed, the queues were long, and, as mischance would have it, I found when I pulled into mine that I was exactly parallel with him in his. At such moments, the defeated head stays fixed, rigidly facing front; but, as my wife let down her window to enable the tollkeeper to snatch a king's ransom from her grasp, I heard a piercing cry:

'*Mains sales! Mains sales!*' I turned, albeit stiffly. The Porsche driver was grinning at me through the lead-rich gloaming.

'Dirty hands?' I murmured to my wife. 'I thought I knew every translingual insult in the AA handbook.'

'He's not pointing at you,' she said. 'He's pointing at himself.'

I risked a second glance. The grin broadened. The string-backed leather finger jabbed towards its owner's nose.

'*Ni gel!*' he shouted. '*Ni gel!*'

'Nor jelly?' I muttered. 'Dirty hands, nor jelly? What arcane smut is this?'

She offered me one of those looks which only a

quarter-century of wedlock can adequately marinate.

'He appears to be informing you,' she said, 'that he is Nigel Mansell.'

I craned a third time, warmly now, but it was just too late. His tollgate light flicked green, long enough for the Porsche to become a dwindling dot blending into the darkling backdrop of Monaco.

The national pride tempering the private chagrin did not, however, last long. Strolling the shoplit dusk of Monte, I was drawn to a window filled with Union Jacks which, on closer peering, proved to be the backdrop for the serried faces of the House of Windsor. This, though, was no fawning *bienvenue* to UK tourists, nor leitmotif for some *Semaine Britannique* set up to sell cricket bats and bagpipes to the gullible Frog.

As we crossed the street towards them, the beloved faces gradually grew more grotesque until we hove to, finally, alongside what might have been a clip from *Spitting Image* excised by a nervous IBA. For what gazed out at us from the French window were 200 pairs of satirical shoes, somewhat low in cordial intent. Each set of twinned toecaps had been sculpted in plastic to a grisly caricature of a royal couple: for less than a tenner a foot the French were being invited to slop around in Andrew and Fergie, Charles and Diana, and even HM the Q and her great consort. For some not immediately apparent reason, Mr and Mrs Mark Phillips had been spared this ghastly ignominy – mayhap the Princess Royal's unstinting work on behalf of Save The Children had paid off in more ways than one. Who can say?

Who could say anything? The filthy place was shut, and the penalties for heaving a monarchist brick through a Monégasque window are probably severe, so there was naught to do but fume, and slink away.

And take some tiny comfort from the fact that their own royal family is called Grimaldi, so what else could one expect from a bunch of clowns?

Offering Prince Rainier the benefit of the doubt, it may be that the bicentenary of the French Revolution is being allowed to express itself in generalized anti-royalism, albeit of a less vicious strain than heretofore, and the Prince would interfere with cobblers at his peril.

He could end up beneath the guillotine; if only a chocolate one. For, at an enormous *confiserie* nearby, we found ourselves before a bicentennial display of the most unsettling denticidal gew-gaws it has ever turned my stomach to witness. Not merely chocolate guillotines, but marzipan heads redly severed at the neck, and little scaffold-baskets of cream-filled torsos. God alone knew what celebrant horrors they had inside. If ever you doubted that history's tragedy is doomed to repeat itself as farce, come to Monte Carlo.

There is no greater irritant for the temporarily expatriated hack than the absence of his reference books. Were I to have permanently resited myself in St Paul de Vence, instead of being perched here for a couple of nights, I should have brought with me all those dog-eared tomes upon which I have come to rely both to shore up a memory doomed to irremediable decay and also to enhance my faltering tropes with bright borrowed plumes whose provenance, cannily concealed, none but the most suspicious reader could possibly twig.

As it is, I sit here like Rupert Brooke, sweating and hot, not only unable to remember whether there is a t in Gran(t)chester, but utterly unable to find out. True, two boisterous chambermaids are chucking laundry around my hotel room, but they give scant signal of useful familiarity with English Edwardian verse. I could well be wrong, of course – one never knows – but I shrink from investigating.

'*Connaissez-vous* Le Vieux Vicarage, Gronshestair? *C'est une poème de Rupert Brooke. Je voudrais bien savoir si Gronshestair a un t dedans – deux t's, en effet, je sais qu'il y en a un au bout du mot, mais c'est le premier t dont je m'occupe, le t – s'il existe – entre le n et le c.*'

We could all go mad.

Not that I actually want to know how to spell Gran(t)chester, I was merely comparing my situation, you understand, with young

Apollo, golden-haired, whoever it was who described him that way (Eddie Marsh? E.M. Forster?), if it was indeed Brooke who was being described; the chambermaids probably wouldn't know that, either. Or, dear God, what I now find myself desperate to remember, which is what the E stands for in E.M. Forster. I know the M is Morgan, but . . .

'*Excusez-moi mesdemoiselles, mais connaissez-vous E. Morgan Forster?*'

'*Quoi?*'

'*Forster.* Une Chambre Avec Un Vue?'

'*Monsieur veut une chambre avec vue?*'

'*Non, non, j'aime cette chambre, c'est terrifique comme chambre, je ne veux que de savoir le premier nom de E.M. Forster. Petit homme, moustache, espèce de pansy, King's College, tout ça?*'

What ghastly and excruciating traps one falls into! And to think that all I am endeavouring to do is explain to you how it was that I came to meet M Eugene Boudoncle, Inspector of Secondary Schools for the Var, and movie buff.

Yesterday, we were lolling, oiled up, by the hotel pool, watching the sun burn the mist off the distant Mediterranean and smugly congratulating ourselves on the cheering news gleaned from a quidsworth of Tuesday's *Times* that it was cold and wet in London, when, as so often happens in April with the curious micro-climates of the Alpes Maritimes, a small cloud suddenly burgeoned on the hill behind us and great gouts of warm rain began to slap down, churning the pool to foam and driving everyone inside – with, of course, the exception of a couple of middle-aged Germans, clearly loath to yield the beachhead they had risen at dawn to establish.

Instead, they put up a bright beach umbrella, in the briefly startling orange-and-gold colours of the MCC. We wriggled into our bathrobes, ordered coffee and cognac, and watched them from the lounge. The rain became tropical, until, at last, they too chucked in the sodden sponge, and began to make their grudging way into the hotel. It was as they approached the lounge doors that the rain sluicing off the terrace-roof suddenly welled to a continuous stream that struck their brolly like a cataract.

'*Singing In The Rain*,' said my wife. And I, as that most ineradicable of film-sequences sprang into my head, made the terrible mistake of thinking for a moment, and then saying: 'What was the name of the girl with Gene Kelly and Donald O'Connor? Not Cyd Charisse, the other one? Short girl, bobbed hair, dimples?' My wife thought for a bit. 'I can't remember,' she said.

Somehow, I knew she would.

They didn't know in Reception, either, and it wasn't the sort of query with which to break the ice with other guests: you would have to try to spot Gene Kelly fans, and get into conversation on some other topic, and work the conversation round to Great Musicals of Our Time, and if you were wrong about their being Gene Kelly fans you could well be stuck with them, and if you kept on doing it you could well end up stuck with the entire hotel population, and still be no wiser.

But the thing grated in my brain like grit in a sock. There was nothing for it but to drive into Vence and find a bookshop. But when I asked for books on American movies, heads shook; so we turned for the exit. Whereupon a stocky little customer of perhaps 60 excused himself and inquired, in English, if he could be of any assistance. Unhopefully, I explained the problem; and he said, instantly, 'Debbie Reynolds'.

So we all went off to drink, and discuss the cinema, and it transpired that M Boudoncle's favourite comics were The Three Stooges, and I made a firm promise to write to him after we got back to England. Not simply because we liked him enormously, but because, while we had no trouble with Mo and Curly, none of us could remember for the life of us what the third Stooge was called.

Thankfully dehovered, and hurtling back along the A20 from Folkestone last Friday, I spotted a monitory roadsign. '*Tenez la gauche!*' it cried from its prominent pole, '*Links fahren*! Drive on the left!' How wise, you in your turn will cry, clever old Bottomley, sensible old Channon! That is because you do not know where I spotted the sign: just outside Harrietsham. Harrietsham is 30 miles from Folkestone.

What had all our continental visitors been doing up to that point? As first man off the Folkestone blocks, eager for bill-piled doormat and rancid pinta, I had no idea of what might have been going on behind me. Were the ditches full of horribly foreshortened Peugeots and BMWs? Were bemused French and German families dragging their battered bags hither and yon across the tarmac in search of a hard shoulder to cry on? Were rubicund Kentish coppers even now peering uncomprehendingly at alien licence and insurance certificates, while plump farmers' wives filled teapots and tore sheets into bandages?

Still, there's a limit to the amount of time a chap can spend worrying about hapless foreign johnnies on the very eve of the Summer Game. And what better way could there have been of repledging one's cultural oath after a fortnight's unfaithful browsing and sluicing at the Froggy trough than by waddling, last Saturday, through the Grace Gate on the opening moment of the cricket season?

The waddle itself is essential. It is part of the MCC ritual. Even the skinny must essay to affect it, plunging their hands deep into roomy trouser pockets, widening the seat, splaying the legs, thrusting out the belly, and rolling off on that ponderous circumnavigation of the concrete perimeter of the Lord's stands which is what the British have instead of the Rialto and the Corso and the Bois de Boulogne.

It is a promenade not a whit less dandy. Never think for a moment that the insouciance which appears to have lain behind the dawn toilette was anything of the sort. Every loose thread of this apparel is calculated. These trousers have been meticulously baggied, these club ties have been expertly frayed and stained according to ancient craft and custom, the bespoke tailors of these egregiously enormous navy blazers and checked tweed jackets have laboured long and hard at asymmetry and bulge. Even the wiry hair which flares from the empurpled conks has been encouraged to do so, doubtless by a secret mixture of Old Navy Shag and follicular fertiliser made up in some Jermyn Street cellar by masters of the tobacconist's art.

So they stroll and chortle, and their fruity cries trail behind them in clouds of blue pipe smoke, like cartoon balloons. This is Olde Englishe style at its leading edge.

Nor could there have been a finer day for it. The Wodehouse cast had been given a Wodehouse backdrop, a cerulean welkin dotted with fluffy fragments of distant haddock, the spring-green outfield drying under a breeze just strong enough to tremble the cherries on an aunt's straw hat. With the rebuilt Botham waiting in the wings as Worcester went in to bat against the MCC, what more could one have asked?

For him not to have waited there all day, I suppose, while openers Curtis and Lord scraped cautious runs together somewhat on the principle of looking after the pennies and allowing the pounds to look after themselves. Nevertheless, for all the interwicket plodding and the dispiriting sight of premier England bowlers giving nobody any trouble at all, the sluggish activities did produce at least one delightful moment.

Beside me, in the front row of the Mound Stand, sat a tiny boy of perhaps five or six, his father on his other side. With the match well into its fourth hour, Worcester on 130 for no wicket, and quick bowler John Agnew toiling fruitlessly from the Nursery End, the little boy said, 'When's something going to happen, daddy?' Whereupon his father replied: 'Any minute now. Agnew's trying to get a wicket especially for you.'

At the end of the over, Agnew trudged down yet again to field on the square leg boundary, an arm's length from where we sat. Indeed, a small arm's length. The little boy, with that infant temerity which unclad emperors risk at their peril, suddenly reached out and tugged at the great man's sweater.

'Are you trying to get a wicket especially for me?' he piped.

The two metres of Agnew looked down at him, sighed, and offered a smile somewhat wintrier than the day. 'No,' he said. 'I'm trying to get a wicket especially for me.'

There is only one other thing I wish to record about Lord's, and that is that its tuck shop is the only place I know where the jelly babies still have faces. They have noses and ears, as they did when I was young, and for one who had naturally assumed that such fiddly sculpture had fallen into desuetude along with so many other ancient crafts, it was a cheering moment to fork out 60p and find oneself with a bagful of homunculi intact in everything that propriety allowed.

Quite why Lord's should be so favoured, I can only guess. Might there perhaps be a confectioner who specializes in schoolboy nostalgia to the carriage trade? Across the road from the tie-frayers' premises, say, and the factory where elderly ladies sit carefully battering panama hats?

An unsettling moment last Saturday morning, fraught with imponderability, and still vibrating. En route to a fellow sentimentalist who has taken a cottage on Boar's Hill to enable him to wallow in the nostalgic view without actually having to descend into Oxford and remind himself what 30 years can do to towns and paunches, I could not resist stopping off at the King's Arms, my old college neighbour, to stick the memory in gear for the upcoming reminiscent lunch.

Needless to say, the dear old stewe had been comprehensively sacked by Attila the Brewer: felled in the ergonomic interest, the internal walls had gone, along with the rancid Axminster, and the sag-seat chairs and the little wonky tables, the last ha'penny had been shoved and the last skittle tumbled to make way for whooping fruit machines and intergalactic ordnance, and where Sunlight cheese once sweated and fat flies strolled on scabby bangers and serried jars of pickled eggs and walnuts stood like the unspeakable detritus of Victorian surgical ambition, a spotless acreage of multi-national provender now lay, spread out before the humming microwaves.

The place being so altered that it was impossible to populate it with remembered faces, I drank up quickly and, pausing only to mutter *Eheu fugaces*! in order to prove to myself that four years had not been entirely wasted, I was walking briskly out when I happened to catch the eye of a man with his head inside one of those telephone domes. Even through the distorting perspex, it was a familiar eye. It was also an eye that clearly recognized me, though with no surprise at all. He merely put his hand over the mouthpiece, leaned out, and said: 'I'll be here next Saturday', and went on with his phone conversation.

I walked up South Parks Road, racking. A mite too old for a contemporary, what was he? Or, more to the point, what had he been, then? A don? A maunciple? A scout? I took the grey out of his crinkled hair, removed a chin or two, painted over the busted veins, but still it would not come. It was not until I was halfway up Hinksey Hill that it struck me, and the car wobbled.

In the summer of 1960, with the gulf beyond Final Schools gaping, I had toyed with several advertised prospects of employment, and the man on the phone had interviewed me in response to one such application. We had met in that same pub and engaged in a conversation of such ambiguity that its very vagueness should have alerted me to its nature long before I actually asked him if what the Government wanted me to be was a spy.

Despite the allure of, as I recall, £900 p.a. before stoppages, and the engaging prospect of my own hollow tree and ginger wig, I did not become one. Nor did I think any more about it until last Saturday; since when, however, I have been able to think of little else. Is the man not only still in the King's Arms but still in the same game? And if so, then where might I stand, now, or, where, rather, might I deviate?

At 50, one hefts the dice in the hand as the last throw beckons, and cares a little less whether they might be loaded. True, the tacky revelations of the last three decades have left scant romance in the trade, but might there nevertheless not still be a sloe-eyed siren or two out there, bucketing across Europe on the Orient Express with blueprints Sellotaped to her pellucid skin, eager to engage a cynical, life-pitted, deceptively unyouthful but unquestionably attractive member of Her Majesty's Secret Service in a little amusing subversion?

At the time of going to press, I have not yet decided whether or not to return to Oxford next Saturday. This afternoon, I shall buy a fawn trenchcoat and a brown homburg, and if they look good on me, anything could happen.

By then, if the warm weather continues, my contact may well be sitting outside, rendering covert whispering and the passage of invisible ink more difficult. In London at least, this sudden spring has seen an unprecedented burgeoning of not only pub-tables spilling out on to pavements, but restaurants similarly extending themselves towards the kerb.

Chunnelmongers and other pan-Europeans will doubtless take this as encouraging evidence of the internationalizing of the island race, but I fear our domestic temperament has some way to go before it adjusts fully to the al fresco mood of Champs Elysées and Via Veneto.

Last Monday in Marylebone I saw a young couple, sitting at the pavement table of an Italian restaurant, suddenly confronted by an elderly operative pushing a council dust-cart. The young couple pointed out that they were eating, and the sweeper pointed out that he was sweeping. At this point, the three were joined by a waiter, who pointed out that he was waiting, and a manager who pointed out that he was managing. This pointing out rose rapidly to a climax, but it was only ever going to end one way. The young couple stood up, and the waiter and the manager carried the table inside.

The triumphant sweeper looked at me. 'You wouldn't believe the by-laws I could have quoted,' he said.

Yesterday I bought a new car. It was Wittgenstein's 100th birthday. I did not, of course – lest logicians among you begin rooting around for distributed middles – buy the car for Wittgenstein, who hasn't needed a car these 38 years past. I bought it for me. Indeed, even if Wittgenstein were still the holder of a current licence, I should not have bought him a car, because the last time anybody gave him anything he immediately gave it away again, demonstrating that a genius and his money are soon parted. On that occasion it was his father's fortune, which he doled out to Trakl and Rilke to enable them to gobble caviar while versifying. I should not want to see Ted Hughes barrelling around in my shiny new banger. If the Laureate has a fancy for alloy wheels, let him write commercial jingles like everybody else.

I shall return to the wheels in a bit. If, that is, they're still there.

For the moment, you will be burning to know whether there is anything more in the relationship between Wittgenstein and my new car than the mere coincidence of April 26. I am here to serve you right.

When I ordered the car, in February (q.v.), I requested a radio; yesterday, there it was.

'One Pioneer KE 3060B,' said the dealer, ticking his dispatch sheet. 'Detachable.'

'What?' I said.

'It comes out,' said the dealer. 'It is an anti-theft measure. Also stops the bastards smashing the window. Park the car, take the radio out. Bastard looks in, all he sees is the gap where the radio was.'

'I don't want to carry a radio about,' I said.

'You don't have to,' said the dealer. 'You lock it in the boot.'

I thought for a moment. A bit longer, perhaps, than Wittgenstein would have needed to, but not much.

'Hang on,' I said, 'When the, er, bastard sees the gap where the radio was, won't he force open the boot where the radio is?'

'He won't know you're not carrying it about,' said the dealer.

'He can find out whether I am or not by forcing open the boot,' I said.

'You could always leave it where it was and chance him not knowing it's detachable,' said the dealer.

'Then wouldn't I be better off with a non-detachable one he'd have trouble getting out?'

The dealer looked at me, and he looked at the radio, and he coughed.

Whereof one cannot speak, thereof one must be silent (Wittgenstein).

Instead, he drew my attention to a small key on the car's bunch.

'Another security item,' he said.

'Oh good,' I said.

'You will have noticed the alloy wheels?'

'Very attractive,' I said.

'Especially to bastards,' said the dealer. 'Which is why they are now fitted with rimlocks. The wheels cannot be nicked unless they are unlocked with this key here.'

I heard – how can I describe it? – the faintest susurration, as if a Viennese ghost were passing.

'Why,' I said, a nanosecond before I could manage to bite my tongue out, 'don't you fit a lock to the radio, then?'

'That wouldn't stop 'em,' said the dealer. 'They'd just go around with a bunch of keys.'

'Don't say it,' murmured Wittgenstein, but it was too late.

'Then I suppose the best thing to do with the wheels, after you've parked the car,' I said, 'would be to lock them in the boot.'

Some days, when you see where logic gets you, you can understand why Wittgenstein chucked in the sponge and became a gardener.

An hour later, a grasp of mathematics second only to Ludwig's own took me on to the M25. Here is why. My new car is a very quick car, but for 2,000 kilometres it has to be a very slow car. The police will show no interest in me for 1,250 miles. The car has to be run in before I am.

The M25 is exactly 125 miles round. Since 10 circuits of it would therefore do the job not only with peculiarly satisfying arithmetic neatness but also at a salutarily constant 55mph, and since the road's circularity would ensure (unlike, say, driving to Inverness and back) that I could, if cruising palled, exit at any point and never be more than an hour from home, I set off at 9.30am with a view to a gentle circuit before settling down to peck this out of the Olivetti. Do that twice a week, and the car would be race-fit in no time.

It all went so well that I was back at Potters Bar before noon; and, like a kid on a dodgem, sore tempted to another six penn'orth. I was skirting Theydon Bois for the second time, when I became aware of a police helicopter above me. It fell in just behind. The day being fine, I had put the hood down, and I have to tell you that there is little more unsettling than being dogged by Aeroplod at 1,200ft. What were they after?

Which is when it occurred to me that they had probably never seen anyone going round the M25 twice without stopping. What, they were doubtless wondering, is the logic of this situation?

They had, of course, no way of knowing that, had I stopped even for a moment, bastards would have had my wheels and radio before you could say Jack Wittgenstein.

MAY

L et me heartily recommend *Broadcast News*. A little corker. A rattling good night out. A treat for film fans from nine to ninety.

Not, mind, that *Wall Street* isn't almost as enjoyable. You will not go far wrong with *Wall Street*. Slick, sharp, pacey, and with a quite stunning bravura performance from Michael Douglas. On a par, I feel, with Sean Connery in *The Untouchables*. As for *Withnail and I* and *Moonstruck*, you will come out cheering from both. That, you will cry, is what cinema is all about. Would I say these were masterpieces? I might not go that far. I might prefer to reserve that accolade for *The Empire of the Sun* or *The Unbearable Lightness of Being*. Although I do, of course, appreciate that for many filmgoers, *The Last Emperor* unquestionably takes this season's cinematic biscuit.

Not that I have seen any of them.

I planned to see them this May Bank Holiday, or even one of them, but nobody would let me in. I telephoned fourteen London cinemas, but nobody wanted to know. Some that I could not reach by phone, I drove to, but the answer was the same. Clear off, sunshine. Please do not ask for a ticket as a refusal often offends. Do not force us to let the dog out. Do not make us whistle up the Old Bill. Left outside, watching the cheery queues shuffling forward in the cultural van, sharing in the great celluloid renaissance, all I could do was echo Henry Vaughan's plangent mutter of, as I recall, last December: '*They have all gone into the world of light, and I alone sit lingering here.*'

All I had asked for was a seat in which I might smoke.

These have now disappeared entirely. When I first became hooked on cinema, that other addiction was not merely tolerated, it was enthusiastically encouraged. Indeed, the two drugs were symbiotically enmeshed: not only could you smoke in any part of any cinema, the intermission advertisements urged you to leap from the crimson plush and replenish your nicotine stocks at the kiosk. Furthermore, the heroes with whom you identified in the smoky dark, and the heroines for whom you were encouraged to yearn, could hardly play a scene without lighting up. Most of the seminal lines of cinema were delivered while clouds plumed simultaneously from the nostrils just above. To rapt youth, this defined adulthood. Who knows, perhaps if, in *Now, Voyager*, Paul Henried had not lit two cigarettes and passed one to Bette Davis, but instead offered her his half-licked wine gum, the whole history of modern coughing might have been different.

For me, this teenage imprint, eagerly stamped upon me by The Management, has meant that for the past thirty years I have not been able to watch a film without smoking. For the past dozen, creeping apartheid has meant that I have been driven into ever-smaller enclosures as the cinema progressively eroded the freedom it once offered, but I have still been able to see the view, as it were, from the back of the bus. Since Christmas, however, the ban would appear to have become absolute. The cinema is now closed to me. It is a lesson to all persecuted minorities: yield an inch, and there will be 'ell to pay.

I do not know what the answer is. Health fascism is in the saddle, and the Curreys are booted and spurred. And please do not plague me with po-faced correspondence about what is intolerable for you or good for me, I am well aware that I am killing all of us. If there were any mercy upon which I were going to throw myself, though, it would come from the cigarette manufacturers: since they seem to sponsor everything else, might they not be persuaded to build a few comfy smokatoria, somewhere beyond the pale, in which hapless addicts could be shown the latest films? I do not, you will notice, ask the government to subsidise this, in the way that they subsidise other minority needs. After all, I have paid them hardly more than £10,000 in tobacco tax over the years, and you don't get much for that, these days.

While the splenetic dander is up, let me get something else off my wheezing chest.

At 4.40 *a.m.* on Sunday, I dialled 142 with an urgent directory enquiry. It was engaged. It remained engaged, through a dozen attempts. At 4.55, I rang the operator in the hope of being patched through, but the operator could not raise them, either. So I knocked the pillow about a bit, and stared at the ceiling.

How could this be? While I have long grown used, since privatization, to being unable to contact directory enquiries during the hours in which they might expect to be needed, how on earth could they be permanently engaged on a Sabbath dawn when they are needed hardly at all? However skeletal the staffing, it must surely be able to cope with a demand this minuscule?

The only possible explanation is that thousands of subscribers unable to get through at any other time set their alarms at 4.40 am on a Sunday expressly in order to try to prise from directory enquiries the numbers over which they have been frustrated all week. They squat there, crust-eyed and bristled, struggling to muster enough spittle to lick their pencils and dialling their forefingers raw in the battle for information.

It's really rather impressive that, despite this tenacity, British Telecom still manages to remain one jump ahead of them.

Perhaps I ought to start reading horoscopes. Had astrology been my habit, the words '*Watch out on Monday for a tall dark dog. It will leap up at you on the corner of Edgware Road and Sussex Gardens and eat your cheeseburger*' would have alerted me to an unpleasantness which, if it could not have been avoided – the Sign of the Crab is not mocked – could at least have been mitigated. I could, for example, and without smudging destiny's blueprint, have bought two cheeseburgers and eaten one of them before I got to the fateful intersection.

Not being a street-eater (the last time I attempted it I was caned for bringing my blazer into disrepute, and this trauma threaded itself inextricably into my woof), I was carrying the boxed bun back to my car when it disappeared from my hand.

I leapt, and looked down – though not far down, since the thing for which I had unwittingly bought lunch was that rare hybrid, part Irish wolfhound, part Suffolk Punch. There seemed little point in remonstrating with it: there was in its yellow eye something which suggested not only that it had heard all the arguments a reasonable person might offer in these circumstances, but also that the cheeseburger had done little more than whet its appetite for a nice piece of shin.

So I generously allowed it to lope away. It was only after it had gone that I realized that it had not unwrapped the delicacy, it had wolfed – possibly literally; you would have to ask Cruft's – both the polystyrene container and the marginally-less-than polystyrene pattie in a single rabid chomp.

Which observation, a nano-second later, illuminated a bulb above my head which threw a shaft of light so lateral that Edward de Bono himself could have grown warm in its fluorescent glow. For it had suddenly occurred to me that man's best efforts to rid himself of that exponentially burgeoning urban blight, non-bio-degradable junkfood packaging, had all been directed at persuading those who had finished the edible to bin the inedible – but oaf nature being what it is, that will never happen. Therefore, what the Prime Minister's currently flummoxed litter unit should concentrate on is making the containers edible. Now it so happens that edible polystyrene already exists. It is called the prawn cracker. And prawn crackers, I discover, are moulded from vast sheets of material of which the main constituent – having nothing more to do with prawn than a brief contact, late on in its extrusion process, with a sort of crustaceous essence – is in limitless supply.

Clearly, prawn boxes are the answer, and an answer, moreover, which I offer gratis to Mr John Lee, MP for Pendle and harassed Litter Tank supremo, in return for nothing more than a minor gong in the next list. And, of course, a bone for the dog.

This is all quite serious. Even as I write, prostrate senior executives at American Express will be having *sal volatile* poked into their nostrils, Diners will be searching desperately for the Club's black ball, Harrods' internal switchboard will be glowing white with the frenzied calls of assorted Fayeds, and the President of Avis will be setting in train that grim and rarely invoked ritual by which a Wizard Cardholder is formally stripped of those exceptional global privileges which set him apart from the common lessee.

They all think I'm in the slammer. They believe I am a resident of Her Majesty's Guest House 'Wayland', which enjoys fine views over Griston, Norfolk, especially if you stand on a chair. It just shows you what can happen to the milk of human kindness if you don't watch how you pour.

Our story begins with a rare charitable moment in which I donated to the aforementioned chokey a subscription to the world's greatest magazine. I did not at the time appreciate that the WGM's computer would therefore commit me to memory as Alan Coren, Wayland Prison, Griston, Norfolk. This came to murky light only last Friday, whereupon I telephoned the library officer at Wayland, a cheery citizen ever ready to laugh uncontrollably at another's woe, who said that he, too, had been puzzled by the weekly labels, since he had run a forefinger down the guest register and my name was not upon it.

Now, this would not much matter had the magazine not engaged in that barter common to all publications, the exchange of subscription lists. This trade is carried on not merely with other publications but with all sorts of commercial enterprises which carry out their seductions by post. The name thus turns out into an item of electronic currency. Its owner loses all control over it. It becomes The Wandering Name.

So that, any moment now – if it has not yet happened – mine will turn up on files it already inhabits, but with an unsavoury new address; and creditors who have hitherto confidently believed that I hung out in a respectable suburban villa will be offered the unsettling information that I am merely sharing a four-man cubicle. Indeed, there is every likelihood that the Halifax Building Society's computer will come round and take the respectable suburban villa back. The only consolation is that the AA is bound, henceforth, to leave me alone. They do not offer *Encyclopaedias of British Moths* or smart socket-sets to potential customers with an invitation to sample them without obligation in the privacy of their own cells.

I had not planned a penal leitmotif, but this has turned out to be that rare thing for me, a two-prison week. Hardly had dawn risen last Sunday than Mr Melvyn Bragg and I, co-spongers on a delightful country weekend near Winchester, volunteered to pop into the city to fetch the newspapers. That is to say, the Sage of Wigton volunteered, but he doesn't drive. His forte is creative navigation. It is all to do with the disposition of moss, I understand, and a complex bucolic trigonometry involving tree stumps and clouds. Wind may come into it. In any event, the route succeeded in taking us several miles from Winchester before petering out in a rural alley, at the end of which stood a man with a gun. He was not a newsagent. Bragg, though no driver, came up with the smart idea of selecting reverse gear, which at least took us back towards Winchester; but as we rejoined the road, we found ourselves hemmed in by stumbling lines of elderly runners, many in bandages, their eyes rolling, their tongues lolling, and the hedgerows echoing to their plaintive coughing. They were following a distant police car, and another brought up their straggling rear.

'Convicts,' muttered Bragg, and I cannot convey the empathetic agony with which that great humanitarian spirit filled the car. You had to be there. A mile further on, I noticed, on my side, a tiny hand-lettered placard which bore the legend Winchester Fun Run: 3 Mile Mark, but I said nothing. I felt it might ruin Melvyn's day.

What ruined mine, a couple of hours later, was Dr David Owen. He had joined our party for lunch, and when a spot of vicarage tennis was suggested and he gamely agreed to make up the number, I was delighted to find myself drawn against him. Though five days younger than I, he had led, my thinking went, a fraught and debilitating life, particularly of late, which would have left him in no shape to handle The Shot.

I should explain about The Shot. A regular player these thirty years past, to me the whippy drop-shot, the tantalisingly disguised lob, the running cross-court backhand, the blistering pass, have all been cannily eschewed in favour of the ball which hits the top edge of the frame and rockets vertically upwards, leaving my opponent to shower and go home before it comes down again, thus conceding the match.

As it is also a shot designed to flummox the indecisive, I might, I think, have been forgiven for allowing prejudice to persuade me that it was custom-built for an SDP opponent: but I have to tell you that, having been comprehensively, some might say disdainfully, taken apart 0-6 by so seamless a combination of aggression, calculation, commitment and sheer bloody pitilessness, I grieve for the current Cabinet and their myriad groundless dreams of succession.

I know what Mrs Thatcher sees in him.

As 1992 looms, it could well be that Oscar Wilde's observation that America and Britain were two nations divided by a common language will, along with so much else, have to be Euromodified. For, as he might further have remarked, to jeopardize one special relationship may be regarded as a misfortune; to jeopardize two looks like carelessness.

Franglais is now the culprit, and even though the blame should be laid squarely on the Frenchman's unending quest for the linguistically chic – very odd, incidentally, that he can simultaneously hoot at England's style, while deploying its vocabulary to demonstrate his own – finger-pointing does not get anyone very far. A mere 22 miles lands you in the kind of trouble where its source becomes irrelevant.

Arriving in Calais last Friday afternoon in desperate need of tennis balls (and somewhat riskily ignoring the provocative niche they occupy in the history of Anglo-French relations), I looked for a sports shop. In Boulevard Jacquard I found one. How could I miss it ? It was called *Athlete's Foot.*

Inside, furthermore, and in order to negotiate my path to the counter, I had to pass two racks of brushed-cotton track-suits. Each had a placard over it. One rack said *Le jogging.* The other said *Le sweat.* I was fingering both in the hope of discovering the difference between the genres when an assistant approached, shot a charming smile, and complicated things yet further.

"M'sieu," she enquired, *"cherche un track?"* I shook my head, bought the tennis balls, and was on my way out when I spotted a display of elegant white sports socks with a little floral motif on the ankle. The sign above them said *Trés Soxy!*

The potential divisiveness does not, of course, concern comprehension, but pronunciation. Whose word is it, now? Does the Englishman take the tongue that Shakespeare spake, stick it in the roof of his mouth, and — simpering slightly, perhaps, through his meticulously pursed lips — enunciate *le wikkend, le gollkippaire, la perpmusique?* Or does he instead stoutly insist upon that root pronunciation doomed to be construed by his hosts as either ignorance or chauvinism, or, most probably, both?

Then again, it could always be that the shibboleth is *chauvinism* itself: pronounce it with an *e* on the end and you could very likely get away with anything.

It is harder than ever, mind, to determine, in this bicentennial year, whether or not Nicolas Chauvin is the hero he once was or the joke he subsequently became. It could well be that his Republican fanaticism is regarded by some celebrants as unnecessarily restrained. On the other hand, the headline *Princess Di — Est-Elle la Marie Antoinette de Nos Jours?*, above a surprisingly sympathetic defence of royal frivolity, strongly suggests that France is undergoing pangs of nostalgic regret. As revolutionary fervour, albeit ceremonially, once more enthrals the Frog, it is not always clear which way he is going to jump. A counter-revolution could well be on the cards.

In Epernay, last Saturday, we found ourselves caught up in a wildly enthusiastic commemorative procession, tumbrel after flower-decked tumbrel of flush-faced tinies variously clad as aristos and peasants cheerily shoving one another under rickety cardboard guillotines for the delectation of a hysterical crowd, while cannons banged, balloons flew, and tricoloured confetti filled one's underwear.

Unquestionably, it was the midget noblefolk who were by far the most popular, especially with the teenage sections of the crowd. Is this merely youth's natural predisposition towards nonconformity, or the sign of some more deeply atavistic mood?

There is probably no need for François Mitterrand to start worrying until the Paris School of Economics offers the union presidency to Louis XVI.

All that had gone before was nothing compared to the problem of engaging French dogs in small talk. Billeted at the Hostellerie du Château in Fère-en-Tardenois, and taking advantage of the warm weather to ravage my liver *al fresco*, I was well into a second bottle of the local *bouzy* — and Franglais-speakers may make of that what they wish — when a young Alsatian bounded up to my garden table and stuck his nose on my knee. Young Alsatian dog, that is.

No problem at all, nice to be liked by dogs, but after a while I found I could not refill my glass because the hand I use for bottles was in the dog's mouth. Not being bitten, you understand, just being affectionately held. Being gnawed a bit, perhaps, but nothing serious. Since I speak good dog, I not unnaturally assumed I could also get by in *chien*.

'*Assieds-toi*,' I said sharply. Since nothing happened, it occurred to me that I had perhaps been a little informal, so early on in our acquaintance. Thus '*Asseyez-vous!*' I cried. Without letting go of my hand, the dog put its paw in my lap. Where it might very well still be, had M Blot, its owner, not at that moment materialized from his establishment, and shouted '*Seet!*' which it did.

Once the dogs speak Franglais, there's no going back.

Once upon a time (when books began that way) publication day was the day when books began. Chaucer would, without any preamble save the scribbling, blow the blotting sand off *Troilus and Criseyde,* murmur "Go, litel book!", nudge it down the slipway with no more fanfare than one would accord a Pooh-stick, and wait for people to come up to him in the street and say it wasn't half as good as *The Book of the Duchess,* what a disappointment, could they have their groat back.

These days, publication day seems to be the day when books end. Today is the publication day of my daughter's first book, and everything that would appear to have been required of it has already happened. The book has done its job. It has been serialized in national newspapers both daily and Sunday, it is being reprinted before a single copy of the first edition has been sold, and the fecund tot has featured in umpteen press and broadcast interviews, with the result that her prime joy last evening was not excitement that everything was at last about to begin, but relief that everything was at last about to be over.

This made me, for my part, somewhat moody. Not because Victoria and *Love 16* have been conjoined, willy-nilly, in the smooth industrial process which successful publishing has unquestionably become (and some would say about time, too), but, purely selfishly, because I had come to regard the book rather as my first grandchild, an innocent blob to be cradled and cooed over once its mother had counted its pages to reassure herself that they were all there. I thought I would look after it. I thought I would take it into the park and wait for other grandparents to come up and say what a nice book it was, did I think it took after me at all?

In the event, what the stork has dumped beneath the gooseberry bush this morning is a strapping new-born adult, fully kitted out with hair, teeth, and a confident street-wise smile which testify to its having knocked about a bit and seen a thing or two. It is a book of the world.

Some of which explains why I'm even happier than the author herself to see the back of the last camel in the PR caravan disappearing over the horizon. These have not been easy weeks for literary grandparents, especially the one still trying to earn an unpromoted crust at the domestic typewriter. You pop out for a jar of Tipp-Ex, and when you come back home again, the house is full of stubbled things in stone-washed dungarees dragging cameras and microphones about.

"Sorry, Victoria darling, can we take that last bit again, some nerd just walked into shot. Oh Christ, now he's trying to use the phone, will someone *please* tell him we're waiting for Jameson to call back..."

Worse, is being used. "Well, now he's here, why don't we stick him in the background, sort of doting father, all that, could he be cooking something or reading Victoria's manuscript, he looks so bloody inert just kind of, you know, grinning, has anybody got any pancake, I'm getting terrible flaring highlights off his head..."

Worst, is not being used at all.

"Good afternoon, this is the *Wogan* office, this is the *Sunday Times,* this is Andrew Lloyd Spielberg, we are enquiring about the possibility of an interview, an article, a speech, a musical comedy based on..."

"Oh, really, well I'm a bit tied up at the moment, got a 200-word book review to do for *Diesel News,* but I could no doubt find the odd..."

"Who am I speaking to? Is Victoria Coren there? Are you her agent?"

I am not, you understand, part of this circus. I have no intention of promoting The Book, despite its being out, a snip at £6.95 from all good bookshops, and, by the sound of things, coal merchants, family butchers, gunshops, St Botolph's Mission to the Hittites, and anywhere else with a bit of shelf and a till.

My intention in fact, is not to promote Victoria's first book, but Mary Archer's. I just couldn't think of a way into it. Mary's book is called *Rupert Brooke* and *The Old Vicarage, Grantchester,* and is so good that if it were any better it would be nearly as good as Victoria's.

The Archers threw a splendid tea-party for it on the shimmering lawn of the Old Vicarage itself, now theirs, last Friday. Guests were asked for 2.50pm, of course, which meant that when we arrived Mary wasn't there but in front of the church being photographed, because the clock stands not any more, it waits for no man.

Indeed, according to her book, it never stood at ten to three at all, it conked out at a quarter to eight. Amazing what writers used to get away to with — you'd have thought Brooke would have had a stab at "And is there honey on my plate?" or something, but no, the blighter took the sloppy way out, as usual. Catch Victoria doing that! It would have been up the wooden hill to Bedfordshire double-quick, and no, you can't write another book until you've eaten up all your bread and butter.

We grandfathers know a thing or two about literary discipline.

They are packed shoulder to shoulder, yet their behaviour is impeccable. They are an example to us all.

They are waiting for a bite to eat, in orderly lines, in their innumerable thousands, but they are neither jostling nor arguing, nor — as far as I know — grumbling. Disciplined, patient, silent, shuffling forward with resigned and regimented conformity, they could be filing past Lenin's tomb. If, of course, they were not bright green.

Because they are bright green, though, they will have to die. for what they are queuing to eat, on every stem on every bush, is my roses. A week of warm weather has simultaneously set the table and whetted the appetite. I no longer have a garden, I have a vegetarian brasserie, and business is booming. Word has got round. It is standing room only. Everyone has turned up.

Except the Ladybirds.

This absence would not matter a whit, had we not become green ourselves. A few years ago, we should have been out there with the rest of the 17th/21st Herbaceous Borderers, pesticidal tanks strapped to our backs and the barrels of our syringes glowing white-hot; but not any more. Eco-conscience hath made cowards of us all, and we no longer fight our own battles, we rely on mercenaries, and for the last couple of years, the Ladybirds have done a fine job. I endow them with the capital initial, because that is how I have come to think of them: a crack fighting unit with, like so many before them, an ironic *nom de guerre* which belies their true grisliness. Ready at a moment's notice to wing in, seek, and destroy, they are the helicopter gunships of the coleopteric world, able to land on a sixpence, totally committed to one task only, and tooled up with mandibles whose rate of fire can account for a thousand greenfly a day.

Sobering, for us ecophiliacs who — even as we cheer and throw our hats in the hair and run beside the liberating columns as they yomp towards the sound of the roses — wonder whether the greenfly, had they the choice, would not rather be zapped by anaesthetizing pirimicarb than chomped to a ghastlier oblivion by the red berets.

As Kermit the Frog so imperishably sang, it's not easy being green.

Whoever you are.

But this year, the Ladybirds have not shown. Beleaguered, Cricklewood scans its skies in vain. If you are very still, you can hear a billion greenfly chewing.

What could I do but dial 584 8361?

'Ladybirds?' replied the Royal Entomological Society. 'Is that us? I've only been here a week. Can I put you through to the Registrar?'

'Accountancy and law are my specialities,' said the Registrar. 'I am not on the insect side of things. Ring the Natural History Museum and ask for — hang on a minute — Mr Rose.'

Mr *Rose*? Can it be true?

It is true. Mr Rose is the NHM's ladybird man.

'Unkempt ground, is what you want,' said Mr Rose.

'Wasteland, you mean?'

'To the naturalist,' said Mr Rose sternly, 'there is no such term as wasteland. Property developers say wasteland.'

'Forgive me,' I murmured, in as undespoliative a tone as I could muster. 'Is there any particular type I should look for?'

'London,' said Mr Rose, 'supports two principal ladybirds, the 2-spotted and the 10-spotted, each some 4 millimetres in length. You may also find the 7-spotted, but this is altogether a bigger beast.'

'A bigger beast?'

'Could be up to 6 millimetres,' said Mr Rose.

I liked the sound of it. A tank. A T-34 bug. An aphicidal Hoover.

171

'Should I look for —' this part would be tricky: I hardly knew the man '—breeding pairs?'

'Difficult,' replied Mr Rose, 'for the layman. There are minute abdominal differences: you would have to turn them over, but to the untrained...'

'Say no more,' I said. 'I shall simply bag as many as possible. How should I go about that? Is there, er, bait, or...'

'You do not, I imagine, have a beating tray?'

'A what?'

'Quite. Then you must do as Victorian entomologists did. You must use an umbrella. When you have found a bush with ladybirds on it, simply open the umbrella and place it upside down beneath the bush. Shake the bush, and when the ladybirds fall into the umbrella, close it, and take them home.'

Mr Rose is an expert's expert. Even as I scribble this on the fecund banks of the Regent's Canal, the brolly beside me teems. Two miles north, the greenfly munch on, but I shall give them a few more minutes.

That has ever been the last entitlement of the condemned.

We are the Masters now, and a snip it is, at a tenner a nob. Lesser universities may require more substantial testament of magistracy — a plump ream of scribble on *The Deployment of the Semi-Colon in Gammer Gurton's Needle,* say, or *Sources of Agorophobia in the Common Toad* — but Oxford demands as thesis only a dozen words on the face of a cheque to convert boys to men.

At quite literally, a stroke — in this case a bang on the head with a hallowed book — the bachelorhood confirmed 29 years ago in this selfsame building was brought to an end by the Vice-Chancellor last Saturday, and converted to MA. What a satisfyingly concise rite of passage that blow was! Called to the front of the class by the beak, as in the spotty lang syne, I felt that this gentle clout was a symbolic valedictory to all those which had preceded it: I did not, this time, have to show him what I had in my mouth, I did not have to tell him what I had been giggling about, I did not have to explain how a sudden unseasonal gust had sucked my essay through the window, I had merely to kneel and accept as benediction what had hitherto been bestowed only as reprimand. I was a big boy now.

Whereupon I rose from my knees, slow-marched from the broiling Sheldonian Theatre into the marginally cooler quad, slipped like a quick-change soubrette from the white-trimmed BA gown into the red-trimmed MA, filed back inside with my new peers, and accepted the applause of a packed house. Quite what they were applauding, of course, is difficult to fathom; in my own case, the cheers might well have been born out of misplaced pity that it had taken me three decades to scrape a tenner together.

Nor am I myself sure either why I never bothered before or why I bothered now, except that Christopher Matthew wanted to do it, and he didn't want to be the oldest one there. Even then, there was a major sore-thumb element about the serried gathering on the Sheldonian floor: hundreds of young glossy heads, punctuated by two tell-tale blobs, one grey, one bald. Older than the Proctors, older than the Deans of Degrees, and running the Vice-Chancellor himself a bit close for propriety, Matthew and I, our craning wives subsequently confirmed, had had our heads tapped markedly less sharply than our confrères'. Nobody wanted a couple of elderly candidates carried out on a plank .

Once gowned, however, all this changed. When poncing about became the order of the day, the kids were left at the starting-gate. Matthew and I had gravitas. Matthew and I looked the part. Not only did our seniority come into its own, so too did our conjunction. We stalked the touristed streets together, with our hands behind our backs, beaming and nodding. To the casual Nikon, we might have been discussing sources of agoraphobia in *Gammer Gurton's Needle*. Groups from Yonkers and Düsseldorf and Tokyo fell back to let us pass, capturing on slide and videotape the thousand years of academic supremacy we so unquestionably embodied. This winter, we shall be romantic shadows on their domestic walls, while rapt neighbours gawp.

Even the undergraduates could not know for sure. Slice him where you will, there is no student so arrogant or blasé that he cannot be momentarily discomposed by a brace of hooded gowns suddenly materializing in his boozer and swivelling their distinguished heads like Tank-54 turrets, one eyebrow raised, perhaps, one lip a little pursed.

It was good in the King's Arms. I saw one kid take his hand off his girl friend's thigh.

Caped crusaders is what we were, though which was Batman and which Robin you would have had to have been inside our egos to determine. This was our town. When we said jump, the masonry shook.

'It's only eight quid to hire the gear,' murmured Matthew in Wadham garden, after a couple of sunbathers had grabbed their shirts and scuttled back to their rooms to graft at essays from which bogus hay-fever could now no longer excuse them.

'I hear you,' I said. Toughness makes me terse.

'We wouldn't do it often,' said Matthew.

'Once a month?'

'Sounds about right,' said Matthew.